EDITOR
Susan E. Laemmle

MANAGING EDITOR
Hara E. Person

BOOK REVIEW EDITOR
Laurence Edwards

POETRY EDITOR
Adam Fisher

EDITORIAL BOARD
Alan Berlin, Jonathan M. Brown, Paul Citrin, Benjamin David,
Andrea Goldstein, Paul J. Golomb, Karyn Kedar, Richard Levy,
Dalia Marx, Michael Shire, David E. Stern, Michael A. White

PRODUCTION
Publishing Synthesis, Ltd.

COPY EDITOR
Michael Isralewitz

CCAR ELECTED OFFICERS
Ellen Weinberg Dreyfus, President
Jonathan Stein, Vice President
William I. Kuhn, Financial Secretary
Richard A. Block, Treasurer
Debra J. Robbins, Recording Secretary
Shira Stern, Membership Secretary

CCAR RABBINIC STAFF
Steven A. Fox, Executive Vice President
Deborah Prinz, Director of Program and Mentor Services
Lennard Thal, Interim Director of Placement
Hara E. Person, Publisher and Director of CCAR Press

Arnold I. Sher, Director of Placement Emeritus (1989–2008)
and Interim Executive Vice President (2005)
Paul J. Menitoff, Executive Vice President Emeritus (1994–2005)

PAST EDITORS
Abraham J. Klausner * (1953–58), Joseph Klein* (1958–64),
Daniel Jeremy Silver* (1964–72), Joseph R. Narot* (1972–75),
Bernard Martin* (1975–81), Samuel E. Karff (1981–84),
Samuel M. Stahl (1984–90), Lawrence Englander (1990–93),
Henry Bamberger (1993–96), Rifat Sonsino (1996–2000)
Stephen Pearce (2000–2003), Jonathan A. Stein (2003–2009)

*Deceased

CCAR Journal
The Reform Jewish Quarterly

Contents

FROM THE EDITOR
At the Gates — בשערים 1

ARTICLES
Introduction: Jewish Perspectives on Finances and
  the Marketplace.. 3
Karyn D. Kedar

Full Faith and Credit: Jewish Views on Debt
  and Bankruptcy.. 7
Edward Elkin

Housing Transactions, Transparency, and Halachah:
  A Proposal 23
Jonathan Cohen and A. Brian Stoller

Tzedakah, Recession, and Social Policy 45
CCAR Responsa Committee
Mark Washofsky, Chair

The Rabbi as Philanthropic Advisor........................ 59
Ellen Flax

Ethical Priorities in Giving Tzedakah...................... 69
Ruth Adar

The Biblical Debtor's Release (Deuteronomy 15:1–3):
  Bankruptcy It Isn't—Or Is It?........................... 79
Robin Nafshi

Money, Schism, and the Creation of American
    Reform Judaism. 90
Dan Judson

The Decline and Fall of the Interest Ban 103
Hillel Gamoran

POETRY
In the Black Night
Vayishlach. 113
John L. Rosove

BOOK REVIEWS
**The Legacy of Our Reform Kibbutzim: Can We Renew
    the Dream—A Review Essay** 117
    *Light in the Arava? Yahel: Dialogue and a Joint Undertaking
    between the Kibbutz Movement and the Reform
    Movement*
      Gidon Elad
    *Zion in the Desert: American Jews in Israel's Reform
    Kibbutzim*
      William F. S. Miles
Reviewed by Debra Goldstein

Jewish Law in Transition 123
Hillel Gamoran
Reviewed by Herbert Bronstein

An Unsettling God: The Heart of the Hebrew Bible 126
Walter Brueggemann
Reviewed by Mordecai Schreiber

The Sights Along the Harbor 129
Harvey Shapiro
Reviewed by Adam D. Fisher

*The Modern Men's Torah Commentary: New Insights
    from Jewish Men on the 54 Weekly Torah Portions* 131
Edited by Jeffrey K. Salkin
Reviewed by Jeffrey Brown

The Passionate Torah: Sex and Judaism.................... 137
Edited by Danya Ruttenberg
Reviewed by Ruth Gelfarb

Join the Conversation!

Subscribe Now.

Engage with ideas about Judaism and Jewish life through essays, poetry and book reviews by leading scholars, rabbis, and thinkers.

A Journal for All Jews
The CCAR Journal: The Reform Jewish Quarterly
$75 for one year subscription
$125 for two year subscription

For more information and to order, go to:
www.ccarpress.org or call 212-972-3636 x243
CCAR | 355 Lexington Avenue | New York, NY 10017

At the Gates — בשערים

The articles in this special symposium issue represent an innovation on the part of the current editorial board. In most cases, their authors responded to an open Call for Papers.

After reflection and discussion, the board decided to launch symposium issues in this open, public way among CCAR members—and others as well, insofar as the word spreads. Here's how the process works: Once a topic has been selected and guest editor(s) chosen, there's a period during which interested authors can submit abstracts and/or other writing, depending on the editors' needs for the issue. Authors whose submitted material is accepted by the guest editor then prepare full articles.

The *Journal*'s publication calendar now aims for symposium issues about twice a year. The Summer 2010 issue—the next after this one—takes as its theme "Politics and Spirituality: Rabbinic Dilemmas," with Richard Levy serving as guest editor. Plans call for future symposia issues on "Finding Our Path: Becoming a Rabbi After Ordination," "New Visions of Jewish Community," and "Judaism and Science."

The board and I want to receive your suggestions for other topics that might warrant the concentrated focus of a themed issue. We like the interchange between the intensity of such issues on the one hand, and the yeasty mix of "open" issues (like those of Fall 2009 and Winter 2010) on the other.

Overall, we who carry forward the *Journal* on behalf of the CCAR are eager for your articles, poems, and ideas for book reviews. It may help spur your creativity to (re)read the Statement of Purpose that appears among the back pages of every issue. The editorial board reviewed the Statement recently and found that it nicely captures our sense of purposeful publication.

And now, finally, to this issue itself. Its germinating idea arose during a board conference call in February 2009—a few months after the financial crash. I invited board member Karyn Kedar to guest edit the issue; the breadth of her sympathy and understanding, as well as the quality of her writing and editing, will be apparent to, and I trust appreciated by, readers of the following pages.

There's an American novel from 1930 by Michael Gold entitled *Jews Without Money*. Even today, when we know better, its title still jolts us. Rabbi Kedar's introduction to this issue helps us see the economic situation in which we find ourselves more broadly and spiritually.

Of course, neither that introduction nor the articles that follow can directly put bread on the table or a roof over people's heads. But they can strengthen, inspire, and inform us so that we carry forward with greater vigor and intelligence. This issue's fine collection of book reviews, assembled by Larry Edwards, aim at the same positive effects. As a bonus, the poem "In the Black Night—*Vayishlach*," represents John Rosove's first appearance in these pages.

In 1938, the German dramatist Bertolt Brecht forged a "Motto" that speaks to our time and situation:

> In the dark times
> Will there also be singing?
> Yes, there will also be singing
> About the dark times.

Susan Laemmle, Editor

Introduction: Jewish Perspectives on Finances and the Marketplace

Karyn D. Kedar

The world around us invades our sense of blessing with power and drama. We barely settle into the reality of one crisis when the next one invades. It seems that the rules have changed—the banks aren't behaving like banks; performance, ambition, and intelligence are irrelevant to job security; what was affordable in previous years is now out of sight. We are hesitant to give in to a sense of security and optimism. Political power is at once hopeful and shameful. And bad behavior is rewarded by billions of dollars.

So as people of faith, when we find ourselves lost without the markers of normal life, we must go back to basics. In the desert when there are no coordinates, the North Star points north. That's basic navigation. With less money, less security, less optimism, we turn to our North Star, which guides us in our pursuit of the true meaning of life: a sense of life's purpose, our core values, our personal mission, and blessing. The teachings of our tradition enable us to discover and rediscover a path that can keep us steady and grounded when all about us seems to be in turmoil.

The impetus for this symposium journal issue is to go back to basics during an historic moment when the ethical issues regarding money, finances, and business dealings are in question in our country, and indeed in the global marketplace. Through a call for papers we present an eclectic collection of articles that can begin a conversation on how our tradition relates to these issues.

In this issue you will read about debt, the ethics of the current mortgage crisis, philanthropy, the Sabbatical year, usury, a CCAR Responsa on *tzedakah* and social policy, the history of synagogues and money, the ethics of *tzedakah*, and the biblical treatment of bankruptcy.

KARYN D. KEDAR (C85) is senior rabbi of Congregation B'nai Jehoshua Beth Elohim, Deerfield, Illinois.

It is my hope that we continue to turn to our tradition for guidance and understanding as well as broaden the scope to a discussion of the personal lessons learned. This is an opportunity for us to reexamine ourselves. What is our relationship to money and wealth? How does this financial crisis inform our charitable contributions? What are our priorities? When speaking of the acquisition of things and the accumulation of wealth, when is enough, enough?

As rabbis, teachers, and spiritual guides we have the opportunity to offer a spiritual, religious, and ethical response to the crisis and conflict in which we find ourselves due to the ramifications of the financial crisis. This moment is about more than money. It is also about power, character in the face of crisis, abundance and scarcity, and spiritual fortitude.

Prosperity comes from hard work, though hard work does not guarantee prosperity. Wealth comes from a good job, though a good job does not guarantee wealth. Riches come from success, though success does not necessarily make us rich. The equation simply does not work consistently. Be smart, work hard, play the political game, be honest and loyal and savvy, and you still may lose your financial footing. We have lost our focus when we think that the endgame is acquisition of material wealth.

Rebalancing is not just a portfolio strategy; it is also a religious concept. Rebalance. How much of our focus is on the stuff of life and how much on the substance? How much time is spent earning and acquiring and how much time is spent giving and loving? How much thinking is spent figuring out finances and how much thinking is spent figuring out relationships? How open are our wallets; how open are our hearts?

We learn from the prophet Isaiah (1:6–10):

> Their land is filled with silver and gold; there is no end to their treasures. Their land is also filled with idols; they worship the work of their own hands. Enter into the rock; and hide in the dust... majesty is in the greatness of God.

Enter into the rock, says the prophet. Go into the cave that hides the treasures of life, and then hide in the dust for the earth reveals its secrets. True greatness is eternal. Wealth has both tangible and intangible indicators. Love and generosity carry us through the tough times. Nobody stands at your grave and reads the details of your portfolio. Life is judged by giving, loving, faith, and the ability to rebalance when we have lost our focus.

Our attitude about money is so rarely about money. It is more complicated than our bank statements, checkbooks, and portfolios. Money provides for us those things that sustain our living. Beyond that, money is a symbol. It can be a symbol for power, for love, for graciousness, for worthiness. When we enter the symbolic world of money we must do so with a great deal of caution and self-awareness. I believe that it all comes down to a spiritual and psychological attitude toward abundance and scarcity. Do you believe that ultimately, at the core of the universe, there is enough? Or do you believe that there will never be enough? Enough what? Enough love. This simple equation is perhaps the most complicated correlation we have. When there is enough, when we believe in the soul of our soul that we are supported, and have faith in something larger than what we can perceive, and when we can tap in to the love that abounds in the world, then we live abundantly. And when we live abundantly, then all things fall into place, including our attitude toward money.

When we are young we are led to believe that our legacy lies in our successes and our failures. And so life becomes a game, a sort of tally, of victory and failures. We keep score of triumphant moments and try to minimize, leverage, and rebrand the not-so-successful moments. All the while we hope and often pray that the endgame will be to our advantage and we will be proclaimed a great success.

But that is only partially true. Our most abiding legacy lies within the strength of our character. And it may just be an ironic twist of fate that character is best built and measured when we experience failure. Not that success is without its test of courage and integrity. But when we fail—and we all do—we experience a profound moment of loss that is layered and nuanced. In failure we may lose the game we are playing, our work, our livelihood, a relationship, a power struggle. And even more crippling, we may lose confidence, a positive self-image, optimism, stability, or good cheer, which knocks us off balance, off our mark. Herein lies the test of character: in the effort to regain composure, balance, direction, our footing. How we react, respond, and rebound is a measure of our inner strength, our character, our fortitude, our inner vision of what is possible despite the outer collapse of what was. It is in the motion of regaining balance that the strength of our character is formed and forged and molded. This current financial crisis, for many, has been the ultimate test of character. And this crisis, financial and otherwise, can also be a great teacher.

As our world attempts to rebound from the financial crisis and its serious ramifications, we find ourselves in conflict and conflicted. In nature, conflict is not bad but rather beautiful. There is no greater conflict than the relationship between mountain and water that creates the Colorado River. Filled with awe, we witness the force of wild water cut through stone, rock, earth, and mountain to create a force that is at once brutal and beautiful, powerful and compelling. I cannot imagine planet earth without its rivers. I cannot imagine life without its conflict.

What can we learn from conflict when we do not judge it, but rather embrace it as a white water rafter embraces the river through a mountain? The rafter sees the conflict between river and mountain as a challenge to be studied, understood, and respected. The rafter combines skill and prayer, care and risk, strength and surrender, adventure and fun to create nothing less than an odyssey, a hero's journey. And so as we accept conflict, rather than fight it, we become nothing less than the hero of our own story.

I want to thank the contributors to the journal for the wide range of subjects and the diversity of thought. I also want to thank my assistant, Chime Costello, and our colleague Rabbi Brian Stoller for their help putting this issue together.

We have only begun to understand the ramifications of our day. If we use this financial and economic crisis as a creative force, inner strength is our raft and character our oar. Strength will keep us afloat and character will navigate us to resolution.

Full Faith and Credit: Jewish Views on Debt and Bankruptcy

Edward Elkin

The wicked one borrows and does not repay.
—Ps. 37:21

Every seventh year you shall practice remission of debts.
— Deut. 15:1

Discussion of the economic crisis that erupted in 2008 and that has taken such a terrible toll on individuals and businesses all over the world has largely revolved around issues of credit. To what extent did individuals take out mortgages and credit card debt that were beyond their means? To what extent did businesses aggressively market such loans to high-risk borrowers? Should individuals and businesses who are unable to meet the obligations of their loans receive help from the government? How easy should it be for individuals or corporations to declare bankruptcy and thereby gain relief from their creditors and discharge all or part of their debt? Will later generations suffer from massive government corporate bailouts financed by astronomical government debt?

These are but some of the many questions concerning borrowing, debt, and credit that have occupied economists, policymakers, and the general public since this crisis began. Financial and general-interest publications are filled with analyses and commentaries seeking to respond with public policy suggestions designed to avert similar crises in the future.

We in the Jewish community clearly have a huge stake in the outcome of this debate. Many in our community have lost their

---

EDWARD ELKIN (NY90) is rabbi of the First Narayever Congregation in Toronto.

jobs, have had their homes foreclosed, or have seen their retirement portfolios devastated in this crisis. Donations are way down, and our synagogues and organizations have had to make severe cutbacks in staff and programming. The government's ability to sustain the social programs that our community has historically supported is threatened by the declining tax base and ever-expanding needs.

Our Jewish stake in this crisis is not limited to its immediate practical effects. As with every major complex societal issue, there are ethical, spiritual, and halachic components to this crisis as well. Polonius may have considered it wise counsel to "neither a lender nor a borrower be," but from the time of the Bible until today, extending and incurring loans has been a part of the economic life of every society. Credit will continue to be crucial both for individuals and for businesses.

The purpose of this article is to explore the Jewish values at play as we consider our own response to debt, both in terms of how we conduct our own financial affairs and as we consider public policy as citizens of a democratic society. In particular, I will focus on the phenomenon of bankruptcy: What does Jewish tradition have to say about the situation in which a borrower cannot meet his or her obligations? Whose interests does the tradition defend most urgently in this scenario—the creditor or the borrower? And finally, what can a liberal Jewish perspective add to this debate?

I. The Biblical Period

The situation in which a borrower does not have the resources to repay a loan is well known in the Bible. When an Israelite man could not repay, the assumption in biblical days is that he would go into debt-slavery, meaning that he would become an *eved ivri*. Often his wife and children would be bonded into servitude as well. Two biblical texts reflect this phenomenon particularly well. In one, a widow comes to Elisha and tells him that creditors are about to seize her two children as slaves. He miraculously makes enough oil for her to sell to pay off her debt and support her family (II Kings 4:1–7). In another example, Nehemiah, trying to rebuild the community in *Eretz Yisrael* after his return from Babylonian exile, hears the people cry out that they are being forced to sell their sons and daughters into slavery because they have borrowed money against their fields and vineyards in order to pay their taxes and cannot repay the loans (Neh. 5:1–5). He reprimands the nobles and the prefects for calling in the loans they had extended to the poor: "Are you pressing claims on loans made to your brothers?... We have done our best to buy back our Jewish brothers who were sold to the nations; will you now sell your brothers so that they must be sold [back] to us?" (5:8). Ultimately, following Nehemiah's own example, the nobles agree to abandon their claims against the poor.

These texts confirm the fact that debt-slavery was a feature of Israelite life. If a person could not pay his debts, a legal—if regrettable—recourse was for that person to become an *eved ivri*. However, biblical law sought various ways to mitigate the worst features of this kind of servitude. The association of this kind of slavery with the Israelite experience in Egypt was simply too powerful to ignore. In the Decalogue itself, the *eved ivri* is granted the right of Sabbath rest along with every other Israelite (Exod. 20:10). His master's right to beat him is severely limited (Exod. 21:26–27), and fugitive slaves may not be extradited (Deut. 23:16–17). Most importantly, a limit of six years is placed on his years of service (Exod. 21:2).

In fact, according to Deuteronomy, debts are annulled altogether at the end of the six-year cycle: "every seventh year you shall practice remission of debts...every creditor shall remit the due that he claims from his fellow; he shall not dun his fellow or kinsman, for the remission proclaimed is of the Lord. You may dun the foreigner, but you must remit whatever is due you from your kinsman" (Deut. 15:1–3). And even during the period when the debt is owed, the creditor is required to "stand outside" and not enter the debtor's home in order to collect a pledge (Exod. 22:24–26, Deut. 24:10–12).

Biblical legislation therefore recognizes insolvency, and the servitude that could be its result, as a societal phenomenon that cannot be eliminated but whose worst effects must be alleviated. There is some recognition that there might also be a problem with debtors of means refusing to pay their debts; Psalm 37:21 ("The wicked one borrows and does not repay") stands out in this regard. But the bulk of the biblical material on this subject reflects the imperative to protect impoverished debtors, not creditors who are owed money.

Much of the tension in the tradition around this issue stems from the fact that in the ancient world loans were sometimes viewed as an act of *tzedakah* and sometimes as a commercial transaction.

One's attitude toward non-repayment of loans is often determined by which one of these two definitions is primary. In the biblical period, the view of loans as *tzedakah* for the poor predominates, but later on, as commerce develops and the economy becomes more complex, the latter view often prevails.

II. Debt in the Talmudic Period

A full examination of the issue of credit and debt in Rabbinic literature is beyond the scope of this paper. However, two important points must be made. First, the Rabbis establish that the repayment of loans is a positive commandment. This becomes clear in a discussion between Rav Kahane and Rav Papa in *K'tubot* 86a. Both agree that repayment is a mitzvah, a religious obligation. Rav Papa maintains that repayment is also an obligation the violation of which could lead to flogging *ad sh'teitzei nafsho*, "until his soul departs." This discussion reflects the fact that the Rabbis have begun to view debt not just in the framework of *tzedakah* but also as a commercial transaction in which, at times, people of means refuse to meet their obligations.

The other factor from the Talmudic period that must be mentioned is Hillel's *prosbul*. The *prosbul* is often cited in liberal Jewish circles as a precedent for rabbis responding to the changing circumstances of the times. But the actual content of the *prosbul* technique is important for our discussion. Hillel noticed that because of the biblical law of the sabbatical year, which mandated that debts were canceled in the seventh year, people were not issuing loans in the years leading up to the sabbatical year. The Bible had already anticipated this problem when it warned against people withholding loans to the needy as the seventh year approached (Deut. 15:9). However, the problem clearly existed into the Rabbinic period, and exhortations to lend were simply not enough to keep credit flowing. Hillel devised a legal formula that enabled a creditor to still claim his debts following the sabbatical year by giving the bonds to the court prior to the advent of the sabbatical year (*Gittin* 36a). The biblical prohibition against collecting that debt was held to apply to individuals and not to the court, so the creditor would get his money back after all.

The *prosbul* was controversial in its time. Several authorities claimed that they would abolish it if they could. But it is noteworthy that Rabbi Hisda explains the term *prosbul* as being derived from the phrase *pruz buli u'buti* (*Gittin* 37a), meaning that it is an advantage for both rich and poor—the rich creditors got repayment on their loans and the poor had access to much needed credit, which they had hitherto been deprived of in the years leading up to the sabbatical because of the effect of the biblical law.

The Rabbis did, of course, stand by the protections for debtors that they had inherited. Some were even extended. For example, while the Torah prohibits a creditor from entering the house of a debtor to collect what he is owed, the Rabbis say that the prohibition also applies to a *shaliah* (officer of the court) who has been appointed to collect the assets of the debtor (*Bava M'tzia* 113a). The Gemara also explicates what arrangement must be made for the debtor, i.e., what assets he must be left with, even if the creditor or the *shaliah* does collect his assets in order to pay off his debt. This arrangement is called a *sidur l'baal hov*. For example, two couches and a mattress must be left for a wealthy man, and two couches and matting for a poor man (*Bava M'tzia* 113b).[1]

For all these safeguards for the debtor, however, the establishment of repayment as a mitzvah and the institution of the *prosbul* reflect the fact that a new perspective on lending and borrowing had taken root in the Rabbinic period. Whereas the focus in the Bible was on protecting debtors as much as possible given the desperate circumstances of the poor, the Rabbinic period displays sensitivity to the rights of creditors as well, and a recognition of the importance of keeping the flow of credit going—for everyone. Not all debtors were in fact poor. Some were people of means who did not want to repay their loans. A new system that balanced the needs of creditors and debtors had to be devised.

III. Maimonides

Maimonides builds on his Rabbinic inheritance in the twenty-seven chapters of his *Hilchot Malveh V'Loveh* in the *Mishneh Torah*. The extent of this material reflects the sophistication of *dinei mamonot* in the medieval period and also the complexity of the subject.

Rambam reiterates that it is a positive commandment to lend to the poor and considers this commandment to be even greater than the commandment to give charity—because the person asking for alms has crossed the psychological barrier already and so doesn't suffer as much humiliation, whereas the person asking for a loan has not yet faced that particular shame (*Hilchot Malveh V'Loveh* 1:1). Rambam also says that it is a transgression to press a poor Israelite for repayment if the creditor knows he doesn't have the means (1:2).[2] It is also forbidden for a creditor to frighten or embarrass a debtor (1:3). Debtors may not be imprisoned nor may they be required to bring proof that they are indeed poor (2:1). In all these examples, Rambam is in keeping with the biblical emphasis on protecting the rights of poor debtors.

However, in seeming contradiction to this approach, Rambam also states that "when a lender demands payment of a loan—even if he is wealthy and the borrower is in a pressing situation and struggles to support [his family]—we are not merciful in judgment (*ein mrahamin badin*). Instead we expropriate all the movable property that the person owns to pay the last penny of the debt. If the movable property he owns is not sufficient, we expropriate the landed property after issuing a ban of ostracism against any person who possesses movable property or knows of movable property he possesses and does not bring it to court" (1:4). Moreover, even if a debtor will be imprisoned by gentiles if his property is expropriated by the *beit din*, the court still has the right to expropriate it (1:6)—at that point, the mitzvah of *pidyon sh'vuyim* (redemption of the captive) becomes operative, and the community has the responsibility to try and win his release. However, that fact shouldn't stop the court from implementing the expropriation. If a debtor claims not to have the means to repay, he should be required to take a solemn oath to that effect called an *Ein Li* ("I have no means"). The only exception to the requirement that this oath be sworn is the situation where a debtor has an established reputation for being poor and virtuous (2:3, 4).[3]

Rambam details a few exemptions to the principle of expropriation. The debtor must bring everything he owns to the *beit din*, but he is allowed to keep food for thirty days, appropriate clothing for a year, a mattress, his sandals, and his *t'fillin*. A craftsman may keep two tools. He is allowed to keep only what he needs for himself, not for his family; it appears that this would be too much consideration to ask of a creditor (1:7).

In all these provisions, Maimonides stresses the rights of creditors. By raising the possibility of *cherem* for those debtors who have property that they don't report to the court (2:2), he demonstrates an awareness that sometimes debtors are motivated to hide their assets. A system which is too "kind" to debtors would result in a system where people of means would not want to lend. *Ninalah delet lifnei lovin*, "the door would be bolted against those who sought loans" (2:2). As we have seen, that would be detrimental to both rich and poor.

For Maimonides, the goal is to make as clear and specific as possible how the court should achieve the balance between the competing goals of compassion for the poor on the one hand and maintaining a viable commercial system on the other—a system in which people are deterred from reneging on their debts and lenders are prepared to take appropriate risks and keep credit flowing to those who need and want it.

IV. Imprisonment

While the imposition of slavery as a remedy for nonpayment of debts appears to have faded away in the postbiblical period, a new form of punishment for this offense began to become common in the lands of the Jewish dispersion —imprisonment. This punishment seems clearly prohibited by biblical sources, which don't even allow creditors to enter the homes of debtors. Maimonides specifically outlaws it (*Hilchot Malveh V'Loveh* 2:1).

However, in the thirteenth and fourteenth centuries, as commercial life became more complex, the attitude toward debtors' prison began to change. The responsa literature of the time reflects the fact that evasion of debts and concealment of assets had become widespread,[4] and *poskim* began to take a fresh look at an option that their forebears had taken off the table. Certain scholars remained adamantly opposed to this remedy; Rabbi Solomon ben Adret (Rashba), for example, maintained that even when the contract between the parties specifically allowed for imprisonment in case of nonpayment, that provision in the contract (known as a *t'nai she-baguf*, a condition relating to one's body) could not be enforced, even if the debtor was found to be concealing assets.[5]

Rabbi Isaac bar Sheshet Perfet (the Ribash), however, the leader of the Saragossa Jewish community in Spain, wrote a responsum in which he allows for imprisonment in the case of a debtor of means who has concealed his property, although not for a pauper. He bases his argument on the text in *K'tubot* 86a discussed above, in which the principle is laid out that it is a positive commandment to repay one's debts. In his *t'shuvah*, he lays out the reasoning why imprisonment is actually forbidden. However, he says that the leaders of his local community had issued a *takanat hakahal* allowing it despite the prohibition, saying that there were so many *ramain* (swindlers) that to disallow imprisonment would lead to a complete drying up of credit. So the Ribash found a justification in *K'tubot* 86a to allow both imprisonment and *makkot* (blows) as a deterrence.[6]

Various later authorities disagreed with Bar Sheshet's decision to allow imprisonment of debtors, including Joseph Caro.[7] But in time imprisonment did come to be used commonly as a punishment for swindlers who did not repay their debts (who came to be known as *borhim*). Interestingly, even those *poskim* who maintained the prohibition on imprisonment for personal debt allowed it for nonpayment of tax debts. They were living in an environment in which Jewish communities lived at the sufferance of local rulers; any diminution of tax revenue could mean persecution or expulsion for all. So the punishment in this case had to be severe.[8]

V. Bankruptcy as a Jewish Option

Bankruptcy in modern western societies is a legal means whereby debtors can discharge all or part of their debt. The debt is eliminated even if the debtor later becomes wealthy. The purpose of bankruptcy laws is to allow for an orderly and equitable distribution of assets that remain when a debtor cannot meet his or her obligations.

As outlined by Steven Resnicoff, bankruptcy protection serves several important additional social functions: it allows debtors to have a fresh start, it minimizes the likelihood that debtors will engage in immoral conduct such as stealing in order to survive, it reduces the likelihood that the debtor will go on welfare, it encourages creditors to extend their credit wisely because they know about bankruptcy protection going into the loan, and it encourages entrepreneurs to take out loans necessary to develop their business and thereby grow the economy.[9]

The question for us is whether this remedy may be considered Jewishly valid. As we have seen, Jewish law requires debts to be repaid. There is no provision for discharging debts; in fact, some authorities consider such a discharge to be the equivalent of theft by the debtor. If a debtor can't pay at the time the debt is due, he must repay it when he can. Bankruptcy as we know it therefore simply does not exist in the Jewish legal tradition. Can it be justified?

Resnicoff cites various halachic strategies that have been employed in order to justify bankruptcy in this legal environment. One such strategy is called *minhag hasocharim*, in which local custom is assumed to govern any commercial agreement, even when that custom is different from Torah law on the matter. Since bankruptcy is part of the law of our wider society, it can be halachically justified on this basis.

However, even when bankruptcy can be legally justified, that doesn't mean that the *poskim* approve of it. Rabbi Ezra Basri is an example of a *posek* who agrees that creditors must accept bankruptcy discharges set by secular courts. However, he uses strong rhetoric to denounce those who take advantage of this procedure despite the fact that they are wealthy: "Those who go bankrupt while their homes are full of valuables and do not pay their creditors, even if they do so through secular courts, have stolen merchandise in their hands. They will ultimately have to give an accounting. There is not enough space to expound upon the enormity of their guilt, especially if they do so with respect to non-Jewish creditors, because they profane God's name and cause non-Jews to say, 'this is what Jews do.' One cannot describe the extent of their punishment *(ein l'taer onsham)*."[10]

We can see by the extreme nature of this rhetoric that Rabbi Basri was concerned that allowing bankruptcy on the basis that it is the custom of the society might lead nefarious people to take advantage, a development that must be deterred however possible because it brings Jews into ill-repute among their gentile neighbors.

The general halachic approach to bankruptcy at this point would best be characterized by the term "necessary evil." It is not a solution that emanates from Jewish sources, and so it should be discouraged. But it is an established procedure in the wider society and therefore must be borne.

VI. Reform Movement Approaches

There has not been extensive discussion of commercial matters on the CCAR Responsa Committee. However, in 1961, the committee discussed whether a congregation may use the secular courts to collect delinquent building pledges.[11] It ruled then that such matters should *not* be brought to gentile courts in part because to do so would represent a *hilul HaShem*.

A 2004 CCAR responsum[12] disagrees with the stance taken in the 1961 ruling. While acknowledging that there is a long tradition going back to the Talmud of not relying on gentile courts, the more recent ruling maintains that our circumstances vis-à-vis the wider society have changed so radically that this notion no longer applies: "These are not 'Gentile' courts, but *our* courts, belonging to 'us', just as much as to 'them.' To suggest that Jews should not avail themselves of our nation's courts on the grounds that they are 'secular' or 'Gentile' tribunals is to imply that our legal position in this society is not that of equal citizenship." Similarly, the 2004 responsum addresses the *hilul HaShem* argument, claiming that we no longer need to be excessively fearful of presenting a negative image to the general public because we are now more confident of our position in society.[13]

As a result of this more recent responsum, we can say that the Reform legal tradition would provide no barrier for debtors seeking protection from their creditors in secular bankruptcy court. But the committee has not specifically addressed the legitimacy of bankruptcy in general.

In 2000, the U.S. Congress passed a law intended to tighten bankruptcy laws by subjecting bankruptcy applicants to a means test that would steer most applicants to a much stricter payment plan. At the time, the Religious Action Center urged President Bill Clinton to veto this bill. Rabbi Saperstein explained RAC's position as follows:

> Crushing the poorest Americans beneath unrealistic payment plans would force them to make impossible choices—between repaying credit card debt and feeding their families, between repaying a loan and meeting child support. And since these provisions will particularly hurt divorced families living in poverty, this legislation can only deepen child poverty.
>
> In biblical times, debt-relief was structured into the Sabbatical, or seventh year, remission of debt. It is specifically referred to as "God's remission of debt." *A fair and equitable bankruptcy system plays the same role in our society.*[14]

The language used by Rabbi Saperstein in his criticism of legislative efforts to make filing for bankruptcy protection more difficult makes it clear that he sees lending in the social justice context. Similarly, the resolution on predatory lending adopted by the URJ's Commission on Social Action in 2007 reveals a *tzedakah* perspective. The background paper for this resolution stresses that unfair lending practices affect the most vulnerable among us and mentions specifically impoverished individuals, rural borrowers, people on fixed incomes, women, minorities, seniors, and military personnel. The resolution does use language acknowledging that interest rates should "appropriately recognize the risk that lenders incur" but otherwise focuses on protecting debtors rather than creditors. This emphasis is much more consistent with the biblical approach to lending as an act of compassion than with the more balanced Rabbinic trend that tries to take into account the commercial imperative to keep credit flowing by minimizing fraud and protecting the rights of creditors as well as those of of poor debtors.

As we have seen, there is no single view of bankruptcy among contemporary Jewish legal scholars. The issue is complex because it involves a mechanism of redress that does not stem from within the halachic system itself but rather comes from the outside. Any discussion of the topic necessarily leads to the very large and difficult question of the relationship of Jews to the norms of the wider society in which they live. In the ever-present tension between the rights of creditors and the rights of debtors, secular bankruptcy represents a major shift over to the rights of debtors in that it allows for some debts to be discharged altogether—a measure not contemplated in the halachah, at least not since the biblical remission of debts in the seventh year fell out of use.

VII. Bailouts

Most of our discussion has assumed the scenario of a weak, vulnerable debtor forced to choose between repaying a debt and feeding his or her family. But what if the debtor is a large corporation whose directors and executives knowingly took risks that led the corporation to financial ruin, unable to meet its financial obligations? Even if we feel that there is justice in allowing such corporations to fail, what about all their employees and their families—individuals who were not involved in the big decisions but would nevertheless suffer the consequences of those decisions if the company went out of business? If we say that some companies are "too big to fail," how do we determine which merit taxpayer funded rescues and which not?

This is an area that bears further research. We know that the halachah does allow for individuals to be taxed by the community to further certain social goods. For example, the Mishnah tells us that citizens can be forced to participate in the financing of projects needed for the security and well-being of the town.[15] As well, funds were raised for Torah education, feeding and clothing the impoverished, care for widows and orphans, and the redemption of captives. The collection of funds for building religious institutions such as synagogues, cemeteries, and *mikvaot* was another obligation.[16] If there is Jewish precedent for taxation in order to further the common good of the community, might the well-being of the larger society justify the use of taxpayer funds to bail out corporations that can't pay their debts?

Such a case can be made, especially in a time of high unemployment. A counterargument can also be made, however. It is very tricky to define the larger social good in such situations. Yes, a particular auto worker's job would be saved if her company is bailed out. However, if the government uses its enormous resources to save inefficient or reckless companies, won't the economy as a whole suffer and in the long run, won't many more people lose their jobs as a result? And what about the damage to the public good that is sustained when the government itself takes on enormous debts to finance such bailouts? Are the massive government deficits being accumulated during the current crisis really in the interest of society as a whole?

Meir Tamari makes the case for separating "the demand for charity and righteousness from legal support for creditor's rights" as a way of preventing what he calls "economic immorality."[17] In other words, we shouldn't confuse our *tzedakah* obligations with the need to maintain an orderly market. The market has to operate in accordance with all of its laws and consequences, and if people find themselves in distress as a result, society has to have a robust system of communal support to help those people get through their rough patch. Charity, Tamari maintains, is financed in Judaism through taxation and not as a result of denial of the creditor's legal right to the debt.[18] Public funds should be used for programs such as retraining, unemployment benefits, or interest-free loans for start-ups. Although he doesn't come out explicitly against corporate bailouts, Tamari's description of bailed out companies as "sheltered workshops for the unemployed"[19] indicates that bailouts might not be the best public policy in his view.

Yet it is unclear how easily business and *tzedakah* can be separated. Certainly, Rabbi Saperstein's approach reflects the perspective that the economic system itself needs to be set up in way that reflects the values of justice and righteousness. Allowing business to be business while relying on the communal purse to support the needy would work if business itself worked fairly and justly and provided equal opportunities for advancement. What if the business culture itself, however, is corrupt or oppressive?

Conclusions

The recession has forced us to consider Jewish approaches to some of the major economic challenges our society is facing. These challenges tend to be quite complex and confusing; even many of the "experts" in government and business have been improvising in response to the unprecedented meltdown in the housing and stock markets and the crash of industries like the auto industry, which employ hundreds of thousands of people. If looking at these problems from a purely economic standpoint doesn't yield easy policy solutions, it is even harder to factor in value systems that are external to economics when we consider such questions—such as, in our case, Jewish tradition. Yet that is our job—to apply the wisdom of Jewish sources to the most significant issues we face. I derive five insights from Jewish sources that I see as applicable as we grapple with these questions.

1. Credit is important. Going back to biblical times, potential lenders were warned not to freeze credit out of fear that they wouldn't be repaid. Moving forward into the Rabbinic period, as the economy grew more sophisticated, the rights of creditors not to be defrauded were legally recognized. Without that recognition, credit wouldn't flow—and that would be bad for both those who needed/wanted loans and those who had the means to provide them. Today, our economy is even more complex. But still the imperative to remove

impediments to lending remains. Maimonides' injunction that *ein m'rahamin badin* sounds harsh, but there do need to be rules in place that systematically protect those who are in a position to extend loans.

2. However important the availability of credit is in society, we must be modest and restrained in our use of it. Living within our means and being circumspect in our risk-taking are worthy goals both individuals and businesses should strive for. Financing a flashy lifestyle through easily available credit can lead to disaster. For creditors, the aggressive marketing of credit at exorbitant interest rates to people who clearly cannot afford these terms should be exposed for the social evil it clearly is.

3. There are many good and honest people on both sides of the credit equation. However, there are also creditors who prey on the most vulnerable and borrowers who defraud those who have extended loans in good faith. Our *yetzer hara* is particularly active in regard to financial matters. The temptation to greed is powerful, in both rich and poor. We need to create a justice system that recognizes this essential truth of human nature. If greed leads us down the path to becoming either an exploiter or a swindler, there must be legal consequences for our actions.

4. The bankruptcy system that has evolved in most western countries seems to work reasonably well as a way of balancing the rights of creditors and debtors. Depending on who is in power at a particular time, the system can be tinkered with to the advantage of one side or another, and we must be vigilant about providing correctives if it goes out of whack. It is certainly a more humane way to address the situation of unpaid debt than indentured servitude or debtors' prison. It does not emanate from Jewish sources, but it is nevertheless one of those areas where our halakhic scholars have found ways to accommodate a useful outside innovation.

5. Maintaining a strong social support system is essential. There is no precedent in our tradition for a social Darwinian position in which the poor and vulnerable are left to their own devices. The question is, who should be responsible for their support: creditors (by insisting that they forgo repayment on loans), society at large (through taxpayer-supported social programs or

bailouts), or private charity? If we feel that all have a role to play, how do we sort out the various responsibilities of each? These are challenging questions, but the complexity of the task should not deter us from seeking answers. The sector that we have most direct involvement in and influence over is our own Jewish community, and although we no longer have powers of taxation among our community, at times of economic distress we must redouble our effort to remind our members of their covenantal obligation to help support those in need. Nehemiah used the power of his rhetoric to move his peers to do right by those who were in debt to them; we need similar rhetorical skill today to move ourselves and our community to do right by the most vulnerable members of our society—both in terms of our own *tzedakah* and in terms of our activism on behalf of social programs designed to help the needy. The biblical provision for remission of debt is not legally applicable any more, nor has it been for many centuries. But it should inspire us to support a generous approach when it has been determined that debtors are in fact impoverished.

Although the economic and societal context in which we live today is vastly different from that of our ancestors, they did explore many of the same issues that we face. Their experience and insights can help us work our way through the challenges we face in these difficult economic times in a Jewishly authentic way.

Notes

1. See *Sefer HaTerumot* of Rav Shmuel ben Yitzhak HaSardi for a fascinating discussion about whether a debtor who is a *talmid haham* should be allowed to keep his books. *Sefer HaTerumot leRabeinu Shmuel ben Yitzhak HaSardi* (Jerusalem: Mechon Or HaMizrah, 5748). Shaar Alef, Helek Alef, #8.
2. Interestingly, this provision does not apply to gentile debtors.
3. See Menahem Elon, "Execution," *Encyclopedia Judaica*, vol.6 (Jerusalem: Keter, 2007), 597.
4. See Menahem Elon, "Imprisonment for Debt," *Encyclopedia Judaica*, vol.9 (Jerusalem: Keter, 2007), 748.
5. *Sefer Sheelout u-Tshuvot Ha Rashba* (Jerusalem: Masoret Yisrael, 5760). Helek Rishon, Siman 1069.
6. Daniel Metzger, ed., *She'elot u-Tshuvot Ha Rav Yitzhak bar Sheshet* (Jerusalem: Machon Or HaMizrah, 5753). Helek Sheni, Siman 484.

7. *Shulhan Arukh Hoshen Mishpat* 97:15.
8. See, for example, the response of Rabbi Asher ben Yehiel, in which he bases the imprisonment of those who owe taxes to the king on the principle of *dina d'malchuta dina*. *Sheelot utsvhuvot l'rabeinu Asher ben Yehiel* (Jerusalem: Machon Or HaMizrach, 5754). *K'lal* 68:10.
9. Steven Resnicoff, "Bankruptcy—A Viable Halachic Option?" *Journal of Halacha and Contemporary Society* 5 (Fall 1992): 26–28.
10. Rabbi Ezra Basri, *Dinei Mamonot*, vol.1 (Jerusalem: Ktav Institute, 1985), 68 n.4.
11. American Reform Responsa, no.17 in *CCAR Yearbook* 72 (1961).
12. 5764.1.
13. Having ruled that bringing this case to a secular court is permissible, the committee goes on to discuss whether it is advisable in this particular case, but that discussion is beyond the scope of this paper.
14. RAC press release, May 2, 2000. My italics. Another version of this bankruptcy reform law was passed by Congress and signed by President George W. Bush in 2005. The intent of this law, which was supported especially by the credit card companies, was to cut down on fraud and abuse by making it harder for people to file for bankruptcy and have their debts discharged.
15. *Bava Batra* 1:5
16. Meir Tamari, *With All Your Possessions: Jewish Ethics and Economic Life* (New York: The Free Press, 1987), 213.
17. Meir Tamari, *The Challenge of Wealth* (Northvale, NJ: Jason Aaronson, 1995), 211.
18. Ibid.
19. Ibid., 212.

Housing Transactions, Transparency, and Halachah: A Proposal

Jonathan Cohen and A. Brian Stoller

Over the past two years, the housing-market crisis has led to a significant fall in prices in many parts of the United States and to many people losing their homes. Despite its devastating consequences, however, this recent crisis has not resulted in a thorough examination of the structure of the real estate market and its weaknesses nor has it generated much discussion regarding religious values and obligations in the marketplace. This article seeks to raise these issues and to present a first step towards filling these gaps.

We start by identifying some of the major structural problems that have been highlighted by American experts in the real estate field as sources of market inefficiency. Next, we present halachic material that addresses issues of defects in properties in order to promote the use of halachic principles in comparing regulatory systems and in assessing the religious implications of market operations. At the conclusion of this article we offer a general outline of a proposal for the creation of a halachically inspired submarket in real estate, which we believe would mitigate the inefficiencies identified in the housing market as it is presently structured.

I. Sources of Market Inefficiency

In economic terms, market efficiency is defined as "getting the most out of resources used."[1] According to academic literature, two key factors contribute to inefficiencies, or less than maximally productive

---

JONATHAN COHEN, Ph.D. is associate professor of Talmud and Halachic Literature at HUC-JIR in Cincinnati. He also serves as the director of the HUC-University of Cincinnati Ethics Center.

A. BRIAN STOLLER (C08) is assistant rabbi of Congregation B'nai Jehoshua Beth Elohim in Deerfield, Illinois.

use of resources, in the housing market: (1) information asymmetry between buyers and sellers, and (2) high transaction costs.

A. Information Asymmetry

As the technical term suggests, information asymmetry refers to an economic condition in which certain market participants possess or have access to more and/or better information about the market than do others. Such informational imbalances can distort participants' incentives and contribute to market inefficiencies.[2] Though extant to some degree in every market save the theoretical perfectly competitive one, it stands to reason that the greater the informational imbalance within a given market, the more inefficient that market will be.

A number of analysts suggest that the accessibility and quality of information are important factors in real estate transactions and concur with Cho's conclusion that the housing market is "not informationally efficient."[3] While informational imbalances can vary from place to place depending on the conditions and regulations governing a given local market, information asymmetry in the housing market generally favors sellers over buyers. That the seller's informational advantage is generated by the current structure of the housing market is demonstrated by a number of factors, which can be grouped into three broad categories:

1. General market factors. In a study of information asymmetry in the commercial real estate market, Garmaise and Moskowitz identify two factors that surely lead to similar imbalances in the residential market and may therefore be applied in the present analysis. First, the market for housing, like the market for commercial properties, is "highly illiquid,"[4] meaning that product turnover is low. Since homes sell relatively infrequently, they explain, housing prices are slow in adjusting to reflect current market conditions and therefore lag in conveying information to buyers about both the market and a particular home.

Second, the high degree of heterogeneity in the housing market is a source of information asymmetry. Unlike other consumer goods such as appliances, stereos, and clothing, houses are not mass produced, so no two houses are exactly the same. Moreover, even when two homes are identical in many respects, location is a factor that necessarily makes each house unique.

Consequently, property values are highly dependent on idiosyncrasies such as the particular features of a given home and local market conditions, making real estate "difficult for outsiders to value."[5] Garmaise and Moskowitz contend that sellers are likely to have better information about the various factors that affect property value, such as the value of particular amenities in the context of the local market, the economic and social dynamics of the neighborhood, local government regulations, impending development projects, and environmental factors. Thus the housing market's high degree of product differentiation contributes to a structural information disadvantage for buyers. As will be demonstrated below, the halachic tradition is particularly sensitive to the information asymmetry that arises in markets for heterogeneous "goods," such as animals, slaves, brides, and real estate, and makes significant efforts to mitigate it.

Both the lag in the housing price mechanism and the acute heterogeneity of the housing market ultimately contribute to market inefficiency, as buyers and their agents expend more time and resources bridging the information gap than they otherwise would if they had access to better information. We hypothesize that a more transparent mechanism for filtering market information to buyers would reduce such expenditures, enabling more housing dollars to go into houses, rather than into information-gathering activities. Indeed, one study reports empirical data from Georgia's real estate market indicating that when information asymmetry between buyer and seller was lessened, both buyers' search costs and the average time needed to sell a house declined.[6]

2. Property-specific factors. Another key source of information asymmetry is that sellers generally have more accurate information than buyers do about the condition of the property itself.[7] While sellers are required by law to disclose known defects in the property, they are under no obligation to share other information about the home's general condition that may be relevant to buyers—e.g., that the roof, while in fine condition now, will likely need replacing in a few years, or that a furnace leak, fixed on the cheap, is likely to become a safety problem again at any moment.

It bears repeating that the law requires disclosure only of *known* defects. Sellers are *not* obligated to inspect the home for defects of which they are presently unaware; indeed, they have a financial incentive *not* to do so. For one thing, hiring an inspector costs money. Furthermore, since sellers are legally bound to report all known defects, inspections have the potential to uncover information that may force them to lower their asking price. Therefore, it is financially advantageous for sellers to remain in the dark about possible defects and simply to write "I don't know" on the disclosure form. It behooves them to make the calculated bet that they will attract a buyer who may not discover any defects or who, upon finding flaws in the house, will be willing to buy it anyway and absorb the repair costs. While it is possible that sellers may ultimately have to pay for the repairs after a buyer inspection, it might be worth it to take that risk rather than willingly assume the costs themselves up-front.

Under existing disclosure requirements, nearly all the risk and liability associated with the sale of a home is allocated to the buyer. The information asymmetry that these requirements generate can only have a chilling effect on buyers: Because buyers know that certain vital information about the condition of homes for sale is inaccessible to them—or perhaps even concealed from them—they will certainly be more reluctant to enter the housing market than they otherwise would be if better information were available to them. Moreover, it stands to reason that buyers discount the prices they are willing to pay for houses to account for the significant risk factor associated with purchasing them. It is perhaps for these reasons that, as will be explained below, halachah aims to allocate the risk involved in property transactions more equally between buyers and sellers by insisting on a transparent, verifiable standard for assessing a property's condition. Our hypothesis is that greater transparency with respect to the condition of properties would ease buyer concerns about entering the market and mitigate the risk-based discounts built into home prices, resulting in more home sales and more money in sellers' pockets.

3. Reliance on real estate agents. As Curran and Schrag point out, most buyers participate in the housing market only infrequently;[8] Palm adds that "Gathering information is expensive and time-consuming" and most buyers have limited resources to expend on their housing search.[9] This being the case, typical buyers require expert assistance in navigating the market and acquiring the information they need to make a purchasing decision. Equally important, buyers generally need real estate agents because Realtors enjoy exclusive access to the local Multiple Listing Service (MLS),[10] without which it is very difficult for buyers to find homes for sale in their price range, in their preferred neighborhoods, etc. For these reasons, typical homebuyers frequently rely on real estate agents as their primary information mediators.

Though Realtor expertise can and should ease the housing search process, such heavy reliance on Realtors currently poses a problem because, as Palm explains, real estate agents constitute "a highly structured information source";[11] that is to say, the information they provide to prospective buyers is selective and biased. In an empirical study of two American residential real estate markets, Palm reports that Realtors "tended to over-recommend areas in which they work, in which they list houses, and with which they are particularly familiar."[12] Thus the information buyers obtain from their agents is at best incomplete; at worst, such information may distort buying patterns and compromise the efficiency of the market.

On top of this, the traditional "seller's-agency" system that governs many local real estate markets exacerbates informational asymmetry between buyers and sellers. Under seller's-agency, both the listing agent and the selling agent (the agent who brings the buyer and seller together) bear fiduciary obligation to the *seller* and, as such, they are obligated to share information they know about potential buyers with the seller.[13] Obviously, this system produces an informational imbalance that favors sellers and which, as Curran and Schrag suggest, may distort the market by discouraging buyers from sharing information with their agents about their housing preferences.

Even in markets where a formal seller's-agency system is not operative, the standard system of fixed Realtor commissions as a percentage of the sale price aligns Realtors' personal financial interests with those of sellers, i.e., to encourage buyers to pay as much as possible for a given property. It is for this reason that Garmaise and Moskowitz conclude that "buyers cannot rely on brokers to provide unbiased information."[14]

Curran and Schrag show that when the state of Georgia replaced its traditional seller's-agency regime with a buyer's-agency system—thus rebalancing the distribution of information between buyers and sellers—buyers' search costs declined, Realtors were better able to match buyers with houses that the buyers liked, and the average amount of time needed to sell a house fell.[15] In light of this data, we posit that restructuring Realtor incentives so as to mitigate the information asymmetry agents currently generate would produce similar benefits in other local markets. By enabling buyers to obtain more complete and more trustworthy information from the agents on whom they rely for advice and by creating an environment in which buyers can feel safe communicating their housing preferences to their agents without worrying that doing so will compromise their bargaining power, such a restructuring, we expect, would improve market efficiency.

B. High Transaction Costs

Transaction costs are the costs of buying and selling over and above the price paid for the product itself.[16] In the market for residential real estate, transaction costs include search costs, Realtor fees, attorney fees, inspection fees, mortgage fees, etc.[17] According to researchers, high transaction costs are another key factor contributing to housing market inefficiency. Among all these, however, Realtor fees may be the most significant contributor to high housing transaction costs, and thus they merit some discussion.

Hsieh and Moretti contend that, under the existing market structure, Realtor fees can generate significant economic losses for market participants. Two primary factors account for this. First, Realtors' marketing costs tend to be high because they include not only the costs of selling the property per se, but also the costs of searching for clients. These "prospecting" costs may include expenditures on mailings, park-bench advertisements, promotional giveaways, and the like. Hsieh and Moretti note that while Realtors provide a valuable service for both buyers and sellers by bringing them together, prospecting expenditures have "marginal social value" that is less than the actual costs borne by the Realtor.[18] Moreover, they report that prospecting costs increase as more Realtors enter the market, without providing any additional benefits to their customers.[19] Because these prospecting costs are surely passed on to the principals through Realtor fees, buyers and sellers end up overpaying for a service that generates little benefit for them.

The second major source of economic loss and market inefficiency generated by Realtor fees is the fixed-percentage commission mentioned previously. Because Realtors typically earn 6 to 7 percent of the sale price, there is direct correlation between the price of a house and the amount a Realtor is paid for selling it: the higher the price, the higher the commission. However, note Hsieh and Moretti, "the effort necessary to sell an expensive house may not be much different from that required to sell a cheaper home."[20] Indeed, their data seems to confirm this view, showing that more expensive homes tend to sit on the market for less time than lower-priced homes.[21] It can thus be concluded that the pricing of Realtor services is not properly aligned with the value of those services. The fixed-commission structure cannot help but generate economic losses for market participants, since it forces sellers (and buyers, indirectly) of more expensive homes to pay Realtors higher fees for the same amount of work.

We hypothesize that mitigating prospecting costs and restructuring the Realtor-compensation mechanism to align service price with service value will improve housing market efficiency by reducing transaction costs.

It is not possible to address, within the context of this article, all the main sources of market inefficiency from halachic perspectives. However, in the pages that follow, we will demonstrate that halachah offers an approach to real estate transactions that is worth examining. On the basis of that analysis, we will offer a proposal for a voluntary, halachically inspired regulatory mechanism that we believe would render realty transactions more transparent and less daunting to buyers in general (and to first-time buyers in particular) and reduce transaction costs. It is our contention that these improvements would enable buyers to spend more of their housing dollars on actual houses, rather than on information-gathering and secondary services, and ensure that more of those housing dollars will find their way ultimately into the pockets of sellers.

The next section of this article presents certain halachic notions that are helpful in considering the problem of information asymmetry with respect to property-specific factors, focusing particularly on issues of property defects. We first explore certain issues that arise from non–real estate cases and then turn our attention to additional halachic principles gleaned from cases dealing specifically with residential real estate.

II. Property Defects in Halachah

A. Issues Arising From Non–Real Estate Cases

One of the disconcerting aspects of a property purchase is the consideration of the potential for its hidden defects and their unknown costs. The halachic analysis of the implications of defects, seen and unseen, often highlights one of two distinctions. First, a defect, *mum* (מום), may be temporary, passing, or reversible (such a defect would typically be called מום עובר); or by contrast, it may be lasting, "fundamental," or impossible to repair without significantly altering the whole defective object or property (מום קבוע). A second distinction is drawn between defects or conditions that are visible or apparent (מום שבגלוי) as opposed to those that are concealed from view (מום שבסתר).

Although these halachic distinctions among *mumim* do not specifically relate to real estate, rabbinic courts have frequently utilized them in their analyses of real estate cases. In the Talmud, the art of identifying defects is commonly associated with the selection of animals for sacrifice. For example, in one passage we learn that a shepherd taught Rab how to detect blemishes in animals and determine whether they should be classified as temporary or lasting. Indeed, Rab's expertise was so highly respected, it was speculated that he would conceivably authorize the slaughter of first-born animals having detected and assessed blemishes that were not apparent to others, who were less skilled.[22] The mere suspicion that Rab's expertise might be misused, or that he might not share information regarding defects with others, reflects Rabbinic concern with the credibility of the selection process and preference for a verifiable standard of inspection.

Another Talmudic discussion addresses the importance of identifying animals unfit for sacrifice and weighs the permissibility of tearing off the animal's wool in order to examine a sign or indication of blemish. In this regard, we learn that animals displaying symptoms of trouble are presumed unfit for sacrifice pending the repeated inspection of an expert (מומחה).[23] Thus, under certain circumstances, Rabbinic regulation imposes a higher standard of inspection to prove that an animal is fit for the purpose of sacrifice, and the burden is placed squarely upon its owner to demonstrate his animal's fitness.

The issue of inspection and assessment of blemishes is significant to relations among people as well. Describing the circumstances that would lead to the liberation of slaves, Talmudic sages discuss the implications of the biblical requirement that those whose eyes or teeth are harmed by their masters be released.[24] The specific mention of both eyes and teeth in the biblical text generates the suggestion that its purpose is to cover organs that are part of the human body from birth (like the eyes) as well as organs that are not apparent at birth but emerge later in life (like teeth).[25] This reflects an expansive Rabbinic approach to the owner's liability with respect to property, in this case the slave's body. The Gemara also proposes that, in order to force release of the slave, the harm caused to either the eye or the tooth must be apparent (גלוי) and permanent (here the language used is אינו חוזר), and that the rule may be extended to other limbs and members.[26] One of the issues also addressed regards preexisting conditions: Would a slave have to be released if his eyesight were poor before he was blinded by his master? If his tooth were loose before his master struck it and caused it to fall? These kinds of questions reflect a struggle to identify the causes of harm and to assign liability for injury and disability. Indeed, in this context, the distinction between apparent and hidden conditions or ailments is crucially important.

This distinction is equally important in the discussion of certain physical problems that undermine the legitimacy of marriage arrangements. The Mishnah juxtaposes physical defects or blemishes that would result in the annulment of a marriage once discovered in the bride with those that would disqualify a priest from serving in the Temple.[27] The physical defects that would disqualify priests include a number of apparent features, like deformities to the face, unusually large or small ears, unusually large breasts (that resemble a woman's breasts), unusually sized or shaped genitalia, unusually shaped legs, unusually colored skin, unusual tallness, shortness, deafness, and the like.[28] To this list the Gemara adds excessive perspiration, hairy moles or moles above a particular size, and bad breath, all with specific respect to women.[29] Talmudic authorities further mention other attributes that are deemed defects, or blemishes, in a wife. These include inter alia a "thick" or unpleasant voice, and, again, unusually large breasts. To illustrate what is meant by "unusually large" the Gemara cites Rabbah bar Bar Hannah's eyewitness account of an Arab woman who lifted her breasts across her shoulders, so that they reached behind her back, and nursed her son.[30] The common element in all the defects or attributes listed here is that they are presumed visible or detectable upon superficial examination.

However, the conditions that would potentially lead to the cancellation of a marriage or annulment of a betrothal may be harder to detect. In particular, it may be difficult to determine whether they existed prior to the betrothal or only appeared later. The timing of the diagnosis is relevant to the imposition of the burden of proof, assignment of liability, and placement of responsibility with respect to the "defective bride."[31] Without entering into the halachic complexities of this discussion, we note that Talmudic authorities, commentators, and *poskim* all debate the implications of information asymmetry with regard to the bride and her physical state. Thus, if the physical blemish were visible, the husband-to-be would not be able argue that he did not know about it. Further, if there were a public bath in the town, and the bride used it during normal operating hours, even concealed physical problems would presumably become apparent to the other women who used the facility and by extension to others in the community; as such, they would no longer be concealed. According to certain *rishonim*, a husband's claim that he had not been aware of "defects" under such circumstances would likely reflect the failure to do "due diligence" and collect information about the bride.[32] Following this approach, the groom's argument of mistake in contract would be rejected.

The Rabbinic reluctance to broadly interpret the circumstances and "defects" that would disqualify a betrothal or marriage is understandable. Even for those who regard marriage as a transaction, it is unlike other commercial transactions and ought to be entered into most deliberately and seriously.

Another reason for limiting the annulment of marriages and the removal of women from their husbands' households without the safety net of their *ketubah* is the halachic interest in protecting women. Thus, in a relatively recent case that came before the rabbinical court of Petah Tikva, a claimant argued that his wife misled him and hid her true physical condition from him. It turned out that she could not bear children, nor was she strong enough to do housework. He therefore demanded to be unbound from the duty to provide sustenance to his wife and sought to compel her to accept a decree of divorce (*get*) from him. Should she refuse to accept a *get*, he demanded permission to marry another wife. The panel of rabbinical court judges (*dayanim*) rejected his claim and sided with the defendant. The arguments they cited were that the husband must or ought to have known of her medical condition at the time of the marriage, because medical treatments are generally administered in clinics and hospitals that are open to the public, and peoples' ailments rarely remain a secret. In this respect the defendant was deemed like a bride who had gone to the public bathhouse. In addition, the *dayanim* speculated that the woman's ills may have developed after the marriage and that her husband could not renounce his responsibilities towards her. In short, the onus was on the claimant to establish three things: first, that his wife's medical condition preexisted the marriage; second, that her medical condition was concealed and unknown to him; and third, that his lack of information caused him to enter into a marriage he would otherwise not undertake. In this case, the claimant failed to convince the *dayanim* of all three.[33] Another issue that arose in this case related to the possibility of the wife healing and being able to bear children. She argued that with medical treatment, she stood a good chance of carrying a child to term, rather than suffering miscarriages. In sum, one of the central issues about which the parties argued was the chronic nature, or permanence, of the "defect" or condition that afflicted her.[34]

To summarize: In respect to the various issues surrounding property defects, the foregoing material reveals in halachah Rabbinic dispositions to insist on a transparent, verifiable standard for identifying and assessing defects; to place the burden on owners to demonstrate the quality of their property and its fitness for use; and to expansively assign to property owners liability for defects and responsibility for remedying them. In addition, the halachot regarding marriage demonstrate the Rabbis' willingness, in certain cases, to annul contracted agreements upon the emergence of previously unknown defects.

B. Issues Arising from Real Estate Cases

While halachah allows for the annulment of transactions and the disqualification of animals and people, it must be emphasized that, in the aforementioned cases, it does so only for particular purposes and only in very particular circumstances, which include the emergence or discovery of certain serious defects. Throughout, Rabbinic analysis highlights the significance of three main characteristics of the defect: its nature, the moment of its appearance, and the relevant parties' awareness of it. In cases that involve the breakdown of a marital relationship, the Rabbis typically would be reluctant to exempt a husband from payment of the *ketubah* should he wish to divorce.

By contrast, in certain commercial cases, halachic authorities appear more willing to annul the transaction when defects emerge and to restore the parties to their previous positions. For example, in the context of real estate transactions, the Rabbis assign a great deal of responsibility to the seller, with a view to protecting the buyer. This means that in various cases, instead of renegotiating the deal and ensuring that the costs are allocated appropriately, the Rabbis offer the buyer an opportunity to rescind the contract.

An early statement of principle in this regard is Rambam's pronouncement to the effect that any purchased item (including slaves and real estate) can be returned, even years after the sale, if a defect initially unknown to the buyer is discovered in the item, providing that the buyer ceases to use it once the defect is discovered.[35] Rambam's formulation, which also appears in the *Shulchan Aruch*,[36] marks a radical distinction between the halachic tradition and the caveat emptor nature of American real estate practice.

Yet, the application of Rambam's principle is not always straightforward. In one early fourteenth century case, parties residing in Seville negotiated a transaction involving houses in Cordoba. After the signing of the contract but before the transfer of possession, squatters or vandals entered the houses, destroyed doors and windows, and caused damage to the walls by lighting fires indoors. The buyer wanted to withdraw from the contract, arguing that these defects, which he had not contemplated, rendered the transaction voidable. The seller proposed to deduct the repair costs from the purchase price, on the basis of a professional appraisal. Rabbenu Asher sided with the seller, agreeing that the damage done to the houses was not sufficiently severe to warrant the annulment of the transaction. In his judgment, every house sold could still be called a house in spite of the damage done to it, and the defects in these houses were temporary and reversible.[37]

Additional detail regarding the type of damage or blemish that would render a real estate transaction voidable was offered by Rabbi David ben Zimra (Radbaz): Where the damage or defect was visible and the buyer inspected the house and could see it, it was presumed that he or she was aware of it and accepted the property in its defective state. However, in a case where the damage or defect was hidden or invisible, or if only a very close inspection (by candlelight, such as the *chameitz* inspection that precedes Passover) would reveal it, we would not assume that the buyer was aware of the defect, and the transaction was therefore voidable.

Now, what if the seller offered to assume responsibility for the repair? If the damage were not in the structure of the house (but in an accessible water or sewage pipe, for example), or if it affected an element of the house that was shared with others, the transaction would remain valid, and the seller would bear the burden of the repair. However, the discovery of a defect in the structure of the house, like the finding of a compromised wall, would render the transaction voidable.[38] Here, the rationale underlying this distinction is not financial; in other words, the cost of repair is not the criterion used to distinguish between defects that allow the buyer to rescind a contract and others that do not. Rather, the reasoning is that a change in the structure of the house alters the character, or nature, of the house and turns it into a new, different property (פנים חדשות). The agreement to purchase applies to the old property, not the new one, and cannot be enforced upon the buyer should he or she wish to withdraw.[39]

To illustrate this principle, Radbaz cites an established analogy with a sandal. One Talmudic discussion contemplates the status of a damaged sandal that was rendered impure. As sandals used to have two straps, or flaps, with rings, on the inside and outside of the foot, to hold the laces that would secure the foot, the question was: What would be the status of the sandal if one of the straps broke? The answer was that if the strap located on the inside of the foot broke, the sandal would still be usable, and the lace could be knotted differently (on the inside of the foot) to compensate for this. However, if the external strap broke, the sandal would require a repair that would alter it, and render it a new item. Consequently, the impurity attached to the old sandal would not survive.[40]

Another case recorded by a contemporary of Radbaz involved a house sold by a widow and her son. Before the sale, the seller invited the buyer to enter and inspect the house, and he declined, saying that he was already familiar with it. A contract was made between the parties, and, as agreed, the widow remained in the house for three months before possession would be transferred to the buyer. During this period, the buyer learned that the seller invited a craftsman to install a shelf on one of the walls, and the craftsman refused saying that the walls were unstable and that he would not bear responsibility for any damage done to the house as a result of his nailing or drilling anything to them. It appeared that the foundations of the house were compromised and that gaps in the soil had formed under it, rendering the house dangerous. The buyer, who had not yet paid for the property, immediately turned to the *beit din* seeking to withdraw from the deal, and the widow contested. She argued that the buyer declined the offer to inspect the house and accepted the risks involved when he made the deal. He countered that she did not disclose any of the defects in the house and that her invitation to visit it was reminiscent of some "who praise the merchandise to make it seem attractive so that buyers jump at it." In other words, the buyer argued that the mere invitation to inspect the house did not absolve the sellers of the duty to disclose its defects. This, too, marks a significant distinction with American practice, which places the onus on the buyer to uncover defects. While the matter was in litigation, a fire that had started elsewhere on the street spread among the houses and completely destroyed the house under dispute. The question that arose was: who owned the house? While the issues of possession and payment were central to the decision, Rabbi Isaac also relied on Rambam's halachah, emphasizing that the defects in the house were structural and serious. He therefore placed the onus on the sellers to demonstrate that the defects in the house would not render the transaction voidable, as they sought to extract payment from the buyer.[41]

The cases we have cited so far represent two extremes: In the dispute that Rabbenu Asher addressed, involving damage to doors and windows, as well as cosmetic damage to walls, the presumption was that the damage was not serious, and that the house was reparable. Incidentally, there was no question the seller would bear the costs of repair. On the other hand, the issue that came before Rabbi Isaac related to a structure that was allegedly unsound and dangerous. To complicate matters, by the time the question was sent, the disputed house had been destroyed. Most cases, however, fall between these two extremes.

One such case was decided by the Rabbinical Court for Monetary Disputes attached to the Chief Rabbinate in Jerusalem in 2000. There, the buyer sought to return a recently constructed apartment to the builder, who sold it after mold started appearing on its northern wall. It was discovered that the wall had not been insulated. The builder offered to repair the damage. Prima facie, the *beit din* could select one of two approaches to this issue. On the one hand, to paraphrase Rabbenu Asher's statement, the apartment could still be called an apartment, in spite of the damage to its wall. Furthermore, it was understood that the damage was reparable. On the other hand, part of the structure of the apartment—a wall—was damaged, as opposed to an external element, pipe, or fixture (like a door or a window).

However, much of the court's decision was dedicated to the topic of mistake and to a discussion of its two types: One occurs when a seller misleads a buyer, so that the defective item purchased fits neither its description nor the expectation of the buyer. In such a case, even if the defect can be repaired, the transaction is voidable, because the negotiation and contract are deemed flawed from the start. Another type of mistake occurs when both the seller and buyer are unaware of the defect. In these cases, if the defect can be permanently repaired, the sale contract should not be rescinded. Yet, in certain cases, the repair would alter the nature of the property, and as a result, the deal would be voidable. In the case brought before the rabbinical court in Jerusalem, it emerged that the buyer continued to reside in the property after the defect was discovered and engaged in construction and repair of it. The court's conclusion was that his conduct reflected a sense of ownership and acceptance of the apartment in its defective state. For this reason, the builder who sold the apartment was let off the hook.[42]

Whether or not buyers in the cases cited above were offered the opportunity to withdraw from real estate transactions, these cases demonstrate the willingness of rabbis to protect the buyer at the seller's expense. As we have already noted, in most real estate markets in the United States, the buyer is responsible for inspecting the property and assumes much of the risk should defects be discovered after the closing. This brief presentation of halachic material reflects a willingness to distribute the risk associated with information asymmetry equitably between the buyer and the seller (who is presumed to know more about the property). In halachah, the burden borne by the seller may be especially costly where the discovered defect is deemed permanent. Indeed, even where the defect is temporary, if the buyer refrains from using the property once the defect is discovered, the cost of the repair normally is covered by the seller. We hypothesize that shifting some risk from the buyer to the seller in the U.S. housing market would encourage potential buyers to enter the market and would constitute an incentive for more rigorous disclosure of problems and potential problems in houses offered for sale.

Other sources of inefficiency in the real estate market are also addressed in halachah. Jewish law regulates the role and remuneration of various kinds of agents, describes the duties borne by parties to a negotiation, and offers much insight on pricing and credit. While it is impossible to cover this kind of ground in a short study, the halachic survey presented above does illustrate the relevance and comparative interest in commercial halachic material. Our hope is that it should spur further study of Rabbinic texts with a view to critically examining contemporary market practices.

III. A New Housing Submarket: A Proposal

In its approach to property transactions, the halachic tradition stands in sharp contrast to the approach embodied in current American real estate practices. For instance, halachah places the onus on owners/sellers to disclose defects and to remedy them, while the American practice is to assign the responsibility for uncovering and seeking remediation of property defects to buyers. The halachic tradition favors a transparent, verifiable standard for assessing the condition of property, while the American practice is to leave such determinations to the judgment of whoever chooses to inspect the property. The Rabbis exhibit a willingness to annul a completed sale when serious defects emerge after the fact, in order to protect buyers; by contrast, the American market culture operates on the principle of caveat emptor ("buyer beware"). Because, as noted above, the halachic approach produces a more equitable allocation of information and risk, there is good reason to look to halachah for inspiration as we seek to improve the efficiency of the U.S. housing market.

We do not, however, favor government legislation to achieve this goal. Rather, we believe that a restructuring of the market along our proposed lines can be achieved in the United States voluntarily, because both buyers and sellers stand to gain financially from such a system. To understand how and why, we need only look to the market for used cars.

The housing market is in many respects similar to the market for used cars, particularly in its acute product heterogeneity (like every house, each vehicle has its own history), its informational imbalance favoring sellers (a car's owner, having driven it, necessarily knows more than prospective buyers about the vehicle), its disproportionate allocation of risk to buyers (the used car market is the caveat emptor market par excellence), and its dependence on and incentives to salespeople (a commission-based compensation structure incentivizes car salesmen to persuade buyers to purchase the most expensive car possible). Yet, unlike in the housing market, there has been a revolution within the used car market against the existing structure: CarMax was founded in 1993 in order to make buying a used car a less frustrating and more efficient process by improving transparency, mitigating the risk borne by the buyer, and incentivizing salespeople to serve the interests of the customer. Looking to CarMax as a model, we propose the creation of a similar submarket for residential real estate in the United States that will operate on ground rules inspired both by halachah and by innovations that have improved efficiency in the market for used cars.

We imagine that this submarket would take the form of a "Transparent Housing Register," accessible on the Internet, akin to the MLS. In order to list a house and/or search for houses on the register, sellers, buyers, and Realtors would be required to accept certain terms of participation, outlined below. While extensive research and market testing would be necessary in order to develop and operate this housing register, we envision that, on the conceptual level, the submarket would aim to achieve the following goals:

1. To reduce information asymmetry by promoting a high standard of disclosure and transparency. Taking a cue from halachah, the submarket rules would place the onus on the homeowner for inspecting the property and for demonstrating its fitness for sale. Following the Rabbinic insistence on a transparent and verifiable standard for assessing the condition of a property, administrators of the housing register would develop a clear, comprehensive set of inspection guidelines that must be met by all participating properties. Among other things, these guidelines would mandate that inspection reports identify the character of all defects discovered—e.g., are they structural or nonstructural, permanent or reparable?—insofar as this can be determined. The guidelines would be posted on the Internet, so that all participants could assess each listed property against the same known standard. In order to list his home on the register, a homeowner would first be required to submit his house to an inspection, pursuant to these guidelines, by an authorized inspector. Homeowners would then be required to disclose all the findings of the inspection as well as all records in their possession pertaining to the property's history and maintenance.

By maximizing transparency in the market, these rigorous disclosure requirements would significantly reduce the amount of resources that prospective buyers would need to expend gathering information. As a result, buyers would have more time to look at houses that they might realistically purchase. By allaying buyers' concerns about reserving enough money to repair unknown defects, these higher disclosure standards would also enable buyers to spend more of their housing dollars on paying the purchase price. Furthermore, by mitigating the information asymmetry that causes buyers to fear that sellers might conceal defects from them, we expect that these requirements would make prospective buyers more willing both to enter the market and, ultimately, to purchase a home. Surely, all of these are benefits that would accrue to participating sellers.

2. To reallocate risk and liability more equitably between buyers and sellers. Following the halachic tradition, the submarket would move away from the customary caveat emptor approach to housing by requiring participating sellers to take greater responsibility for remedying defects. In order to participate in the register, sellers would agree to address the defects discovered on pre-inspection, either by repairing them or by granting price reductions. To reduce prospective buyers' exposure to liability for defects that emerge after ownership is transferred, participating sellers would be encouraged to offer warranties, which are already widely used in the current housing market.

Although these requirements surely increase the burden on sellers above that which they bear in the broader market, sellers stand to gain in the end from the reduction in risk associated with buying a home. Potential buyers who might be sitting on the sidelines may be more willing to engage in the housing market if they know that buying a home is less risky. Moreover, because buyers likely implicitly discount the price they are willing to pay for a house to account for the high risk factor, these innovations may have the effect of increasing the prices sellers are able to garner for their homes.

3. To restructure Realtors' incentives and compensation so that they better serve the interests of buyers and sellers. Following the example of CarMax, the Transparent Housing Register would require that participating Realtors accept a fixed commission for selling a home, regardless of the sale price. By preventing the de facto seller-agency system that exists in the broader housing market, this requirement will enable buyers to feel confident that their agents are not pushing the priciest houses on them but, rather, that they are truly helping buyers find the right house for them. This boost in confidence would likely entice more potential buyers into the market and generate more overall sales, since, as the data from Georgia cited above demonstrates, agents in a non–seller-agency regime are more likely and better able to direct buyers to houses they like. We expect that this requirement would also cause buyers' search costs to decline and the average amount of time needed to sell a house to fall, as they did in Georgia. In addition, this alteration in Realtor compensation would bring the price of Realtor services into line with their value. By inspiring confidence in the fairness of the system, this compensation change would attract participants to the submarket and enlarge the pool of potential buyers—certainly another boon to participating sellers.

Though Realtors appear to be the losers in this arrangement, there is actually good reason for them to participate despite the different compensation structure. While Realtors in the broader market expend significant amounts of time and money prospecting and gathering information for clients, our proposed Transparent Housing Register would alleviate some of those costs for participating agents. A certain amount of marketing costs would be borne by the register itself, which, like CarMax, would surely advertise for customers. We expect that such advertising, combined with the appealing features of the submarket, would do much to attract prospective buyers. Therefore, Realtors who choose to participate would have a lesser need to search for clients in the broader pool of potential buyers. Furthermore, the amount of time and money Realtors would need to spend on information gathering would be minimal, as all relevant information would be disclosed on the register and accessible to all.

By increasing transparency and more equitably allocating risk, the submarket aims to create a higher turnover rate in the housing market. Therefore, while agents would no longer be able to count on the sale of one or two expensive homes to generate substantial income, they would benefit instead from a higher sales volume. As CarMax CEO Thomas Folliard has said, "When you set up incentives that align your salespeople with the customer, everybody wins."[43]

4. To limit the potential for price variation and negotiation. This goal is the logical outcome of the previous three. While we do not propose setting fixed prices for houses the way CarMax does for cars, we contend that increasing transparency, more equitably distributing risk, and boosting confidence in the service provided by Realtors will improve the accuracy of the price mechanism, thereby lessening both the need and the ability to haggle over price. To wit, the more known information there is about a product, the more difficult it is for sellers to capture excess profits and for buyers to get "steals." As a result of better pricing and less negotiating, we expect transaction costs to decline, homes to sell more quickly, and sales volumes to increase. This higher turnover rate would, in turn, reinforce the efficiency of the price mechanism by mitigating the information lag that plagues the broader market.

We propose this Transparent Housing Register because we believe that it would enhance housing market efficiency to the benefit of both buyers and sellers. More importantly, however, we present this proposal as a demonstration of how values and principles gleaned from halachah can inform American Reform Jews' thinking not only about real estate, but also about business issues in general. We hope that, with the recent housing crisis as a backdrop, our readers will engage their congregations in a serious dialogue with the halachic tradition and that the ensuing conversations will inspire and empower them to think Jewishly about the commercial activities in which they engage on a daily basis.

Notes

1. Economist.com, *Economics A–Z*, s.v. "efficiency," http://www.economist.com/research/Economics/searchActionTerms.cfm?query=efficiency.
2. Economist.com, *Economics A–Z*, s.v "asymmetric information," http://www.economist.com/research/Economics/searchActionTerms.cfm?query=asymmetric+information .
3. Man Cho, "House Price Dynamics: A Survey of Theoretical and Empirical Issues," *Journal of Housing Research* 7, no. 2 (1996): 167.
4. Mark J. Garmaise and Tobias J. Moskowitz, "Information Asymmetries: Evidence from Real Estate Markets," *The Review of Financial Studies* 17, no. 2 (Summer 2004): 406.
5. Ibid.
6. Christopher Curran and Joel Schrag, "Does It Matter Whom an Agent Serves?" *Journal of Law and Economics* 43, no.1 (April 2000): 282.
7. Garmaise and Moskowitz, "Information Asymmetries," 409.
8. Curran and Schrag, "Does It Matter Whom an Agent Serves?" 266.
9. Risa Palm, "The Role of Real Estate Agents and Information Mediators in Two American Cities," *Geografiska Annaler. Series B, Human Geography* 58, no. 1 (1976): 30.
10. Chang-Tai Hsieh and Enrico Moretti, "Can Free Entry Be Inefficient? Fixed Commissions and Social Waste in the Real Estate Industry," *The Journal of Political Economy* 111, no. 5 (October 2003): 1086 n. 15.
11. Palm, "The Role of Real Estate Agents," 39.
12. Ibid.
13. Curran and Schrag, "Does It Matter Whom an Agent Serves?" 265–66.
14. Garmaise and Moskowitz, "Information Asymmetries," 410.
15. Curran and Schrag, "Does It Matter Whom an Agent Serves?" 282.
16. Economist.com, *Economics A–Z*, s.v. "transaction costs," http://www.economist.com/research/Economics/searchActionTerms.cfm?query=transaction+costs.
17. Cho, "House Price Dynamics," 167.
18. Hsieh and Moretti, "Can Free Entry Be Inefficient?" 1088–89.
19. Ibid.
20. Ibid., 1077.
21. Ibid., 1111. Hsieh and Moretti write: "Figure 10 shows that the cross-sectional relationship between time on the market and housing prices in 1990 is negative."

22. BT *Sanhedrin* 5b.
23. BT *B'chorot* 25a–b.
24. Exodus 21:26–27.
25. BT *Kiddushin* 24b; see Rambam, *Hilchot Avadim* 5:7–9.
26. Ibid.
27. *Mishnah K'tubot* 7:7.
28. *Mishnah B'chorot* 7, especially 1–6.
29. BT *K'tubot* 75a.
30. Ibid.
31. The debate is primarily about the obligation to pay the *ketubah* (BT *K'tubot* 75a–b); The Mishnah (*K'tubot* 7:8) employs a real estate analogy. If the father of the bride can adduce proof to the effect that the ills that plague his daughter occurred following her betrothal, he can argue that it is "the husband's field that was flooded"—שדהו נסחפה—or that it was the husband's property that was damaged by misfortune.
32. See *Tur, Even Ha-Ezer* 39:17-18, and the Beit Yoseph cf.

ומה שכתב בשם הרמבם;בשם הגאונים ומה שכתב.

33. *Piskei Din Rabbanyim* 6:193 (1954:23). For a selection of early rabbinic rulings in this regard see Responsa Rabbi Meir of Rothenburg 4:659; Responsa Rabbi Simon ben Tzemah Duran (Tashbetz) 1:124, 2:138; Responsa Rabbi Solomon ben Simon Duran 1; Responsa Yakhin u-Voaz (of Rabbi Simon and Rabbi Tzemach Duran) 1:109; Responsa Rabbi Hayim Or Zarua 170; Responsa Rabbi David ben Zimra 3:566; 4:124.
34. Ibid.
35. Laws of Sale (*Hilchot Mechira*) 15:3.
36. Ibid., 332:3.
37. Responsa Rabbenu Asher ben Yehiel 96:6.
38. Responsa Radbaz 1:302.
39. For an earlier source see *Mordecai on K'tubot* 292.
40. BT *Shabbat* 112a–b.
41. Responsa Divrei Rivot (Rabbi Isaac ben Samuel Adarbi) 300.
42. *Piskei Din Yerushalayim* 7:95.
43. Michael Myser, "The Wal-Mart of Used Cars," Business 2.0 Magazine, September 1, 2006, http://money.cnn.com/magazines/business2/business2_archive/2006/09/01/8384327/index.htm.

Tzedakah, Recession, and Social Policy

CCAR Responsa Committee
5769.3

She'elah

The CCAR Committee on Justice and Peace has submitted to us the following three inquiries.

Question 1. Does a severe recession affect our approach to public tax policy and our commitment to social services? Some argue that in a recessionary period we need to both cut taxes and services in order to balance the budget, which will affect programs that address poverty and homelessness. Others advocate greater spending and a renewed commitment to the poor, who bear the greatest burden during a recession. How does our legal tradition balance these conflicting influences?

Question 2. How does a congregation balance its budgetary needs with the economic challenges its members now face? Specifically, is fund raising acceptable as people are losing their jobs and homes? And must members be held to their financial commitments and/or pledges made before the recession, as their own financial status changes? And finally, how must a congregation balance its programmatic needs against its obligations to its staff during a recession? Specifically, if choices must be made, must it look to preserve employment of its custodial and secretarial staff first, understanding that they will have the hardest time coping financially, before preserving programmatic initiatives?

Question 3. With regard to individual obligations: May one say "no" to *tzedakah* during a recession?

RABBI MARK E. WASHOFSKY (C80, GRAD87) is chair of the CCAR Committee on Responsa. He is the Solomon B. Freehof Professor of Jewish Law and Practice, HUC-JIR, Cincinnati.

Teshuvah

We write this *teshuvah* in the spring of 2009, a time of great economic turmoil throughout the world. Many individuals have either lost their jobs or live in immediate fear of losing their jobs. Others have been forced to accept reductions in salary, wages, and benefits. Many who have struggled to save for their retirement or for the education of their children have watched those savings melt away in the present collapse of the financial markets. The resulting anxiety is felt in every one of the levels mentioned in these three inquiries: in the arena of government policy; in the sphere of synagogue and other Jewish institutional activity; and in the lives of individual members of our community. It is difficult, at this moment, to imagine a more pressing and challenging reality than the economic crisis we currently face, the deepest such crisis, we are told, since the Great Depression of the 1930s.

In submitting these questions to us, the CCAR Committee on Justice and Peace asks for our help in framing a *text-based* response to this challenge. What manner of guidance does Torah, as expressed through our sacred texts and the tradition of their interpretation, offer to our communities as they struggle through these troubled times? At the outset, we should note the very real limitations upon our ability to arrive at such a response. While we hold our Jewish tradition to be a *torat chayim*, a "living Torah," that speaks to the circumstances of contemporary life, we know that it may not offer clear and certain answers to the financial difficulties we face. We search our classical sources in vain for detailed responses to the mortgage foreclosure crisis, the freezing of the credit markets, the need to stimulate the domestic and international economies, and the appeals for emergency financial support (or bail-outs) for industries, banks, and nations burdened with foreign debt. This is the case, first of all, because our texts were written long ago, reflecting an economic and commercial context quite different from the one that prevails today. More importantly, though, our tradition has historically recognized that decisions touching upon social and economic policy are not to be made by rabbis and scholars of texts and their interpretation. These matters are instead the preserve of the community itself, the lay political structure acting through the agency of its leaders and on the basis of practical wisdom. At the same time, it is not the case that Torah has *nothing* to say. Our tradition is hardly neutral as to the general direction of the policies adopted by communal institutions. On the contrary: the rabbis have insisted that those decisions not transgress against fundamental Jewish moral values. Thus, while acknowledging that the political leadership must wield wide discretionary authority in doing its job, rabbis have long served as a kind of "collective conscience" for the community, acting as a check-and-balance against arbitrary political decisions that would lead to unjust results.[1]

The Responsa Committee sees its role in this light. We wish to know the basic values and general directions—as opposed to any specific policies[2]—that our tradition would require of our communities. In seeking these answers, we will study the Judaic concept—the better word is *mitzvah*—of *tzedakah*. It is under this rubric that our textual tradition works out its understandings of how we are to respond to the issues of poverty and economic deprivation in our community, issues that lie at the heart of the questions that we have been asked. *Tzedakah*, to be sure, is a religious obligation and as such is not the same thing as "policy." Yet precisely for this reason, because it speaks of fundamental religious and moral values, the idea of *tzedakah* can serve as one of those "checks-and-balances" upon a discourse driven entirely or primarily by economic thought and concern for practical political efficiency. Framed in this way, a discussion of *tzedakah* can help focus our attention upon the values that *should* influence our policy decisions, the direction in which those decisions *ought* to take us.

In this light, let us consider some aspects of the *mitzvah* of *tzedakah* that may be of special relevance to our questions. In doing so, we shall try to derive some general guidance as to the best answers to them.

1. *Tzedakah Is a Mitzvah.* As we have indicated, Jewish tradition defines *tzedakah* as a *mitzvah*, a religious duty. As the *Shulchan Arukh*, the most authoritative compilation of the traditional *halakhah*, formulates the rule: "Every person is obligated (*chayav*) to donate *tzedakah*. This applies even to the poor person who himself is supported by *tzedakah*; he is obligated to donate from the amount that is provided to him."[3] Maimonides (Rambam) locates the source of this *mitzvah* in several Biblical verses: "If there is a needy person among you, one of your kinsmen in any of the settlements of the land that Adonai your God is giving you, do not harden your

heart and shut your hand against your needy kinsman. Rather, you must open your hand and lend him sufficient for whatever he needs" (Deuteronomy 15:7–8); and "If your kinsman, being in straits, comes under your authority, and you hold him as though a resident alien, let him live by your side. Do not exact from him advance or accrued interest, but fear your God. Let him live by your side as your kinsman" (Leviticus 25:35–36).[4] The word *chayav*, "obligation," places *tzedakah* in the category of actions that the individual has no choice but to undertake. It is a *chovah*, a duty, and not a free-will gift of the heart. Although it is certainly better to give *tzedakah* willingly and happily (as befits the fulfillment of a *mitzvah*) than in an attitude of reluctance (that would testify that we are helping the poor against our will),[5] we frequently remind ourselves that the Hebrew word *tzedakah* means "justice" and not "charity": if justice is an obligation that demands our compliance, whether we like it or not, then so is *tzedakah*.

To say that *tzedakah* is a religious duty, moreover, is to distinguish it from social or economic policy. Policy, remember, is evaluated by considerations of practicality and efficiency; a religious duty may be incumbent upon every member of the community quite apart from its outcomes. The best demonstration of this is the detail, stated in the *Shulchan Arukh* passage quoted above, that even the recipient of *tzedakah* must give *tzedakah*.[6] The poor person, after all, is one of us, a member of the community defined by adherence to the *mitzvot*; thus, the words of those Biblical passages apply to him or her no less than they speak to the rest of us. How we decide to spend community funds may be a policy decision; that we all must give *tzedakah* is a religious value that must be observed in any event.

2. *Tzedakah Is a Communal Responsibility*. The sources cited thus far speak of *tzedakah* as an obligation incumbent upon the individual. Yet our texts make it clear that the *mitzvah* to aid the poor is too important to leave to individual decision. The responsibility for raising and disbursing *tzedakah* resources rests upon the community, which must maintain the social and political institutions necessary for this purpose. As Rambam puts it: "In every town where there exists a Jewish community, the members of that community are obligated (*chayavin*) to appoint *tzedakah* collectors, well-known, trustworthy persons who shall make the rounds each Friday, collecting from each individual the sum that is appropriate for him to give and that has

been officially imposed upon him."[7] The timing here is no accident: Friday is the day when the *tzedakah* officials wish to distribute funds to the poor to help them prepare for Shabbat. Friday is also the day when the Jews tend to be in the marketplace. This makes them more readily accessible to the *tzedakah* collectors who, as the texts make clear, are not likely to take "no" for an answer.[8]

This communal, institutional responsibility for *tzedakah* entails a wide grant of legal power. As the codes put it, "If one does not want to donate *tzedakah*, or if he gives less than is appropriate for him to give, the court can coerce him—physically if necessary—to give the amount for which he has been assessed. [The court may also] attach his assets and take from him" the appropriate amount.[9] This power of coercion over *tzedakah* is attested in Talmudic law,[10] yet as a number of commentators have noted, it appears to contradict the Rabbinic rule that "the courts do not enforce the observance of positive *mitzvot* for which the Torah specifies a reward."[11] The logic seems to be that the promise of the reward is in and of itself a sufficient incentive for the fulfillment of the obligation, so that no manner of coercive inducement is necessary or desirable. In the case of *this* positive obligation (Deuteronomy 15:8: "you must open your hand and lend him"), the Torah does specify a reward: "for in return [for helping the needy] Adonai your God will bless you in all your efforts and in all your undertakings" (Deuteronomy 15:10). How, therefore, can Jewish law grant to the court the power to coerce an individual to fulfill the duty of *tzedakah*? Various ideas have been suggested as resolutions of this contradiction.[12] The most powerful and persuasive of these, in our view, is that put forth by R. Yom Tov ibn Ishbili (Ritva, 14th-century Spain): *tzedakah* involves "the plight of the poor" (*machsoram shel aniyim*).[13] That is to say, the demand to aid the needy is of such urgency that it overrides the usual rule that commandments that carry a specified reward are exempt from legal coercion. *This* commandment, it would seem, is too important to leave to the whim of individuals; if they do not wish to fulfill their obligation, the court must be given the power to see that they do. It is with this in mind, perhaps, that the tradition declares "the one who coerces others to give *tzedakah* receives a greater heavenly reward than the one who (merely) gives *tzedakah*."[14]

3. *The Administration of Tzedakah*. The tradition makes various provisions concerning the proper ways for *tzedakah* institutions

to administer aid to the poor. From these provisions, we garner a number of important insights.

First, the Torah itself requires that we give the poor person "sufficient for whatever he needs" (*dei machsoro*; Deuteronomy 15:8). The classical sources interpret this demand quite literally: the poor person must be compensated for whatever he or she has lost as a result of becoming poor. "Even if was his custom to ride upon a horse and have a servant lead the way, if he has become poor and lost these things, one is obligated to restore them to him."[15] This, of course, is a standard often impossible to achieve.[16] Funds are not generally available to restore every person to his or her former economic state, and in any event, no individual donor is obligated to shoulder such a burden alone.[17] The point is that the needs of the poor themselves, rather than those of the donors, are central to the fulfillment of the *mitzvah* of *tzedakah*.

Second, the ultimate goal is to eliminate poverty itself. As Rambam famously puts it in his "eight levels of *tzedakah*," the highest level is reached when one helps the poor person, whether through a gift, a loan, a job, or the establishment of a business opportunity, to the point that he no longer needs *tzedakah* in order to support himself.[18] Rambam's language here is reminiscent of Leviticus 25:35, and some commentators have suggested his source for this *halakhah* is the midrashic commentary to that verse: it is better to keep a person from falling into poverty in the first place than to wait until he has become poor to help him.[19] His intent may also be to remind us, once again, of the centrality of the recipient to the *mitzvah* of *tzedakah*: in aiding the poor, we must do so in a way that does not embarrass them or injure their dignity.[20] From this it follows that those who do not qualify as "poor" are not to receive *tzedakah* and thus become an unjustified burden upon the community's limited resources, and the tradition accordingly discusses the appropriate "poverty line" that distinguishes those deserving of assistance from those who are not.[21] Similarly, one's gift to *tzedakah* must not be so large as to drive one into poverty.[22] Thus, while we have seen that even the poor are obligated to donate *tzedakah*, this obligation is annulled when one is so poor that he cannot support himself and his household.[23]

Third, *tzedakah* is assessed according to the economic status of the donor, rather than in the form of a poll tax (an equal donation from all).[24] Greater wealth brings greater responsibility toward the welfare of one's fellow citizens.

4. *Pledges to Tzedakah.* Jewish law understands a pledge to *tzedakah* as a vow (*neder*), a self-imposed obligation that one is duty-bound to fulfill.[25] Moreover, "(o)ne who has made a vow to *tzedakah* is not permitted to retract it."[26] The relevant legal theory is that when one makes a vow to "Heaven"—for example, a pledge to bring a sacrifice or to make a donation to the ancient Temple or to pay a certain sum to *tzedakah*—one effectively transfers to "Heaven" the legal title to that object or sum, just as surely as if one had transferred the physical possession of some object or sum to an earthly buyer.[27] On the other hand, one can go before a court (*beit din*) or before a scholar expert in the laws of vows and seek a release from the obligation through the process of *hatarat nedarim*, in which one testifies that he or she truly regrets the vow and would never have made it had he or she known "that thus-and-such would have happened."[28] In principle, this remedy applies to *tzedakah* pledges as it does to all other vows. However, in an important responsum, R. David ibn Zimra (Radbaz, 16th-century Egypt and Eretz Yisrael) writes that "the scholar who annuls [a pledge to *tzedakah*] deserves excommunication (*nidu'i*)... because he has caused a loss to the poor."[29]

5. *The Duty to Support the Synagogue.* "Any community consisting of at least ten Jews must provide a structure or space in which its members may gather for prayer at the appointed times. This structure or space is called a synagogue. The citizens may coerce (*kofin*) each other to build a synagogue and to acquire a *sefer torah* and the books of the Prophets and the Writings." These words of Maimonides,[30] particularly the word *kofin*, the same term used to denote the power of the community to coerce individuals to donate *tzedakah*, suggest the high importance that our tradition accords to the synagogue and to our duty to support it. If, indeed, the synagogue is regarded as "the Temple in miniature" (*mikdash me'at*),[31] then the community is required to maintain its synagogues just as surely as the people of Israel were required to build the original sanctuary (*mikdash*; Exodus 25:8). This raises the possibility that support for building and maintaining synagogues assumes a higher priority than other obligations,[32] including *tzedakah*. One major authority, R. Yosef Kolon (15th-century Italy) explicitly holds that "the *mitzvah* to support the synagogue takes precedence over the *mitzvah* of *tzedakah*,"[33] and the *Shulchan Arukh* cites his opinion.[34]

On the other hand, the reasoning he uses to buttress his ruling may strike us as forced.[35] Moreover, a leading contemporary halakhist asserts that when Kolon says "the synagogue takes precedence" he is referring not to its building or physical structure but to the *mitzvot* that are central to the life of the synagogue (*i.e.*, prayer and Torah study). It is absurd, this halakhist says, to imagine that Kolon would grant priority to the maintenance of "lavishly appointed facilities" (*binyanei pe'er*) and "luxuries" (*motarot*) over aid to the poor.[36] The scope of Kolon's ruling therefore remains a matter of deep controversy in Jewish law, and it is difficult to derive from it or from our other sources a firm and fixed rule for ranking the priorities of *tzedakah* and the synagogue. Accordingly, the decision in any particular case rests with the judgment of the community and its leaders, who are called upon to weigh both priorities carefully before determining their answer.

In light of this discussion, let us turn now to the questions submitted to us.

Question 1. We are asked "How does our legal tradition balance [the] conflicting influences" of two general lines of policy: fiscal restraint and "a renewed commitment to the poor"? The word "balance" is key here. We do not presume, nor are we professionally qualified, to decide the better economic policy for governments to pursue at a time of deep recession. Economists, as is well known, are deeply divided on this question, with some calling for fiscal discipline and others advocating fiscal stimulus. What we as rabbis are called upon to decide is the course that best reflects our Judaic religious values. And those values teach us, as a community as well as individually, to do *tzedakah*, to undertake an activist and interventionist approach to social justice that stands in at least some tension with the doctrine of fiscal restraint. We know that some economists believe that a policy of tax-cutting and budget-balancing is the best way to aid the poor, since in their view such a policy will lead most quickly to an economic recovery that will be a boon to all. Whatever the truth of these controversial ideas as a matter of economic theory, they reflect an outlook that is the opposite of *tzedakah*, which requires us to provide direct aid in the form of cash and other essentials to the poor. This is not a matter of choice, to be left to our feelings of compassion; Jewish law defines *tzedakah* as a communal, institutional responsibility and provides that the community's institutions may exercise coercive authority in order to collect *tzedakah* from those able to pay it. Nor is it a question of economic efficiency; the halakhic discussion of *tzedakah* defines it as an act of social justice, to be undertaken because it is *right* and not because it increases the sum total of national wealth.

Again, let us be clear: the goal of this responsum is not to make policy recommendations. We acknowledge that our texts do not explicitly require governments to adopt any one particular economic policy. We simply hold that significant reductions in social welfare spending are inherently suspect in the view of a tradition that teaches that *tzedakah*—assistance provided directly to the poor to feed them, clothe them, house them, and help them to find gainful employment—is a *mitzvah*, a *positive* religious and ethical duty. This suggests to us that, in general, the political efforts of our Jewish institutions should be directed toward supporting programs of social welfare spending rather than toward eliminating them. We recognize, of course, the value of fiscal restraint; our tradition, too, bids us to be careful not to spend *tzedakah* funds unwisely and unnecessarily.[37] Yet to the extent that we conclude that a reduction in assistance to the poor will harm them rather than help them, our tradition, which obligates the community to practice *tzedakah*, would urge us to seek a change in that policy.

Question 2. A synagogue exists in order to teach Jewish values and to exemplify them in the way it conducts its business. *Tzedakah* is one of these values, and the congregation must endeavor to fulfill the obligations of *tzedakah* in its actions, even (and perhaps especially) in times of economic crisis. At the same time, given that support for the synagogue is a *mitzvah*, a religious obligation in its own right, a congregation is entitled to raise funds, even during a recession, in order to insure its continued existence. It is no easy thing to locate the proper balance between these two legitimate and potentially conflicting ends. As we have seen, the question of priority—support for the synagogue versus aid to the poor—is a matter of no little controversy in Jewish law. Here, at any rate, is our effort to locate that balance, at least in broad outline.

    a. There is no question that the synagogue may raise funds to support its central programmatic functions, such as worship and education. This must be taken into account as the synagogue considers how it may best fulfill the requirements of *tzedakah* in its budgetary policy. Thus, while a congregation may certainly try "to preserve employment of its custodial and secretarial staff" as a way of supporting the most economically vulnerable among its employees, it need not (and arguably should not) sacrifice its "programmatic needs" in order to do so. Our lower-paid staff should by all means figure prominently in our concern, but the fact remains that *tefilah* and *talmud torah* are the reasons that the synagogue exists in the first place; Jewish life can hardly prosper unless we support them. On the other hand, whatever "priority" the tradition may grant to the synagogue over *tzedakah* would seem not to include the raising of funds for building and expansion projects that are not immediately vital to the central programmatic goals of the congregation. Such projects should be delayed, if possible, until the economic crisis has passed, allowing congregations to direct their efforts toward the more pressing demands of *tzedakah*, such as the retention of staff.

b. While we are entitled to raise funds, we are forbidden to ask for donations from those who tend to give more than they should, whether out of an exaggerated sense of generosity or out of a desire to escape public humiliation.[38] That is to say, we can ask too much of individuals in the name of *tzedakah*, and this is something that we certainly ought to remember when many of our members are struggling financially.

c. A pledge to the synagogue, like a pledge to *tzedakah*, is defined by our tradition as a vow. In practical terms, this means that it is a promise that is taken with the highest degree of moral—and legal[39]—seriousness. Individuals should strive to meet their pledges to the synagogue, even during a recession. However, a serious decline in one's economic fortunes is regarded as valid grounds for annulling a vow (*hatarat nedarim*),[40] and the one who does so is not subject to criticism on the grounds that he or she has caused "a loss to the poor." Congregations should be ready to extend the terms of pledges so that those who are struggling financially need not feel an obligation to pay their pledges now.

Question 3. Tzedakah is, ultimately, a religious duty incumbent upon every individual, including the one who receives *tzedakah*. Accordingly, there is no right to say "no" to *tzedakah*, even during a recession. The gift should not place an unreasonable burden upon one's finances; if the individual's situation is especially critical, the gift can be a symbolic one. But the gift must be made, for we are a community defined by the performance of *mitzvot*, and none among us should be excluded from that community.

CCAR Responsa Committee
Mark Washofksy, Chair

Notes

1. The term "collective conscience" is that of the late Professor Jacob Katz, who argues powerfully against the "romantic conception" that Jewish law, interpreted and applied by rabbinical scholars, governed the political and economic life of the Jews in pre-Emancipation times. Although by and large the Jewish communities of the period did possess juridical autonomy, says Katz, this did not mean the public life of those communities was conducted in accordance with Rabbinic law. The rabbis rather accepted that the communities could arrive at whatever decisions their leaders thought practical and necessary, so long as those decisions did not involve obvious sins or injustice. See Jacob Katz, *Halakhah vekabalah* (Jerusalem: Magnes, 1984), 237–251. The phrase "collective conscience" is at 245.

2. This does not mean that the CCAR and its constituent committees are not entitled to recommend that governments adopt specific economic and social policies. We do this all the time, especially in our social action work, and we rightly regard it as an essential aspect of our rabbinical function. Our point is rather that the Jewish textual tradition, which is the literary basis of our activity on the Responsa Committee, does not necessarily favor one specific economic policy—say, a policy favoring massive economic stimulus by the government—over another. If we wish to advocate for a stimulus, in other words, we can do so on the basis of a conviction that it more effectively achieves the goal of social justice than a policy of budgetary restraint. The pro-and-con argument in that case is governed by pragmatic considerations of economic efficiency. We should *not* claim, however, that the Biblical and Rabbinic sources "require" such a policy or its opposite. Interpretation of those texts, even of the most creative variety, is unlikely to produce a satisfactory answer to the question.

3. *Shulchan Arukh Yoreh De'ah* 248:1.

4. Rambam, *Sefer Hamitzvot*, positive commandment no. 195, and *Yad, Matanot Aniyim* 7:1. This is repeated in *Shulchan Arukh Yoreh De'ah* 247:1.
5. This point is stated most famously in Rambam's "eight degrees of *tzedakah*": the one who gives *tzedakah* with a cheerful face, even though the amount is less than it ought to be, ranks higher on the scale that the one who gives *be'etzev*, with a countenance that displays sadness, anger, stinginess, etc. See *Yad, Matanot Aniyim* 10:13–14.
6. The source for this *halakhah* is B. *Gitin* 7b. But see below at note 23.
7. *Yad, Matanot Aniyim* 9:1. And see at 9:3: "I have never heard of a Jewish community that does not possess a public institution for the collection of *tzedakah*."
8. See B. *Bava Batra* 8b and *Yad, Matanot Aniyim* 7:10: collectors are entitled to accept pledges (*i.e.*, items pawned as security) in lieu of *tzedakah* "even on Friday." The point, notes Rashi (*Bava Batra* 8b, s.v. *afilu be'erev shabbat*), is that on Friday an individual might reasonably claim that he is too busy with his own Sabbath preparations to negotiate his *tzedakah* donation. Thus, the collectors are empowered to accept a pledge "even" on that day, which underscores the importance of *tzedakah* as a Jewish religious value.
9. *Yad, Matanot Aniyim* 7:10; *Shulchan Arukh Yoreh De'ah* 248:1.
10. B. *Bava Batra* 8b: "Rava exercised legal coercion upon Rav Natan bar Ami, taking from him 400 *zuzim* for *tzedakah*."
11. B. *Chulin* 110b. Among these commentators are *Tosafot, Bava Batra* 8b, s.v. *akhpeh lerav natan*.
12. These include (see *Tosafot ad loc.*): a. the "coercion" of which the Talmud speaks is not a legal power but one of moral suasion and condemnation; b. while the Torah does not authorize coercion in a case such as this, the community resolved among themselves to bestow that power upon its leaders; c. the *mitzvah* of *tzedakah* is not only a positive obligation but in fact involves the *negative* commandment of "do not harden your heart and shut your hand" (Deut. 15:7) —and the Torah *does* permit the court to use coercion to punish the violation of prohibitions ("thou-shalt-nots").
13. *Chidushei HaRitva*, *Ketubot* 49b.
14. B. *Bava Batra* 9a; *Yad, Matanot Aniyim* 10:6; *Shulchan Arukh Yoreh De'ah* 249:5.
15. B. *Ketubot* 67b; *Sifre* to Deuteronomy 15:8 (*piska* 116); *Yad, Matanot Aniyim* 7:3; *Shulchan Arukh Yoreh De'ah* 250:1.
16. See *Shulchan Arukh Yoreh De'ah* 249:1: if one can afford it, one gives *tzedakah* "according to the needs of the poor"; if one cannot afford that amount, one gives a fixed portion of one's income.
17. Isserles, *Shulchan Arukh Yoreh De'ah* 250:1.

18. *Yad, Matanot Aniyim* 10:7, the highest level (*ma'alah*) of Rambam's eight levels of *tzedakah*.
19. The commentators are R. David ibn Zimra to *Yad ad loc*. See *Sifra* to Lev. 25:35 and the Gaon of Vilna, *Bi'ur HaGra, Shulchan Arukh Yoreh De'ah* 249, no. 8.
20. See *Beit Yosef, Tur Yoreh De'ah* 249 (in explaining Rambam's "highest level" of *tzedakah*), as well as B. *Ketubot* 67b: if the poor person does not wish to accept a gift, then we call the *tzedakah* a "loan" (for which we might not ask repayment) in order to spare his pride.
21. "One who has enough food for two meals may not take from the *tamchui* ("charity-plate"); one who has enough food for fourteen meals may not take from the *kupah* (communal *tzedakah* fund); one who has two hundred *zuz* and does no business with them, or one who has fifty *zuz* and does do business with them may not take *tzedakah* at all"; B. *Shabbat* 118a and *Ketubot* 68a; *Shulchan Arukh Yoreh De'ah* 253:1. Several medieval authorities suggest that these ancient sums are no longer relevant and that nowadays one may accept *tzedakah* until he has a fund of money sufficient to do business and support himself and his family; among these are the *Mordekhai, Bava Batra* ch. 500. The *Shulchan Arukh* cites this opinion approvingly in *Yreh De'ah* 253:2.
22. One should not give more than one-fifth of his annual income to *tzedakah* (B. *Ketubot* 50a), lest one be forced to seek *tzedakah* from others (Rashi *ad loc., s.v. hamevazbez*). See *Shulchan Arukh Yoreh De'ah* 249:1.
23. *Siftei Kohen, Yoreh De'ah* 248, no. 1.
24. *Resp. Rashba* (R. Shelomo ben Adret, 13th–14th century Spain) 3:380; *Shulchan Arukh Yoreh De'ah* 250:5.
25. B. *Rosh Hashanah* 6a (based upon Deuteronomy 23:24); *Yad, Matanot Aniyim* 8:1; *Shulchan Arukh Yoreh De'ah* 257:3.
26. *Shulchan Arukh Yoreh De'ah* 258:6, ratifying the conclusions of a long line of authorities: R. Yitzchak Alfasi, *Hilkhot HaRif, Bava Kama* fol. 18b; *Tosafot, Bava Kama* 36b, *s.v. yad*; R. Asher b. Yechiel, *Hilkhot HaRosh, Bava Kama* 4:3; R. Shelomo b. Adret, *Resp. Rashba* 3:298; and *Tur, Yoreh De'ah* 258.
27. *Amirato legevo'ah kemesirato lehedyot*: M. *Kidushin* 1:6, *Tosefta Kidushin* (ed. Lieberman) 1:9; B. *Kidushin* 28b and parallels.
28. Rambam describes the process in *Yad, Shevu'ot* 6:1ff.
29. *Resp. Radbaz* 4:134. See our responsum no. 5769.2, "Annulling a Pledge to *Tzedakah*."
30. *Yad, Tefilah* 11:1.
31. B. *Megilah* 29a, from a midrash on Ezekiel 11:16.
32. "Possibility" implies that such is not always the case. For example, the holiness of a *beit midrash*, a place for the study of Torah,

outranks the holiness of a synagogue that is used primarily as a place for prayer; thus, we may turn a synagogue into a house of study, but we may not turn a house of study into a synagogue. See *B. Megilah* 26b; *Yad, Tefilah* 11:14; *Shulchan Arukh Orach Chayim* 153:1; and *Mishnah Berurah* 153, no. 1.

33. *Resp. Maharik, shoresh* 128.
34. *Shulchan Arukh Yoreh De'ah* 249:16 cites Kolon as *yesh mi she'omer*, "one authority holds that…", casting some doubt as to whether R. Yosef Karo, the author of that great code, endorses Kolon's ruling. However, in his *Beit Yosef* commentary to the *Tur*, Karo explains how Kolon derives his ruling from its Talmudic source (see following note) and raises no objection to that ruling.
35. Kolon bases himself upon *Y. Peah* 8:8 (21b). The passage is a difficult one, but most readers interpret it to suggest that support for the sick and for students of Torah takes precedence over support for the synagogue. Given that the passage does not mention "the poor" in this list, Kolon perhaps understands it to mean that *tzedakah* does not come before support for the synagogue. Such, at least, is how R. Yosef Karo reads the responsum (*Beit Yosef, Yoreh De'ah* 249). The problem, of course, is that this is a classic argument from silence: the failure of the passage to say anything about "the poor" may be a coincidence and not evidence that the synagogue enjoys a higher priority than *tzedakah*. At any rate, R. Eliahu, the Gaon of Vilna, is openly skeptical about the proof (*Bi'ur HaGra, Yoreh De'ah* 249, no. 20).
36. R. Shmuel Halevy Wosner, *Resp. Shevet Halevy* 9:199. Wosner argues that Kolon distinguishes between ordinary donations to a *tzedakah* fund and the assistance given to poor persons who are actually in need: the latter is in fact a higher priority than supporting the synagogue, for to aid the poor is a *mitzvah* of the Torah (Deuteronomy 15:7–8). The logic of Wosner's distinction between *tzedakah* and aid to the poor is difficult to fathom, but his position is clear.
37. See at note 21, above. See also *B. Pesachim* 112a and *B. Bava Batra* 110a: one should go to great lengths to avoid taking *tzedakah* (*Shulchan Arukh Yoreh De'ah* 255:1).
38. *B. Bava Batra* 8b; *Shulchan Arukh Yoreh De'ah* 248:7.
39. See our responsum 5764.1, "Collection of Debts to the Congregation" (http://data.ccarnet.org/cgi-bin/respdisp.pl?file=1&year=5764): a synagogue is entitled under Jewish law to sue in civil court for payment of pledges. This right, however, involves a serious threat to the standing of the synagogue as a religious institution; it should be invoked sparingly, if at all.
40. See *Yad, Nedarim* 13:25: it is a *mitzvah* to fulfill a vow to *hekdesh* (the Temple and, by extension, the synagogue) and not to try to gain release from it, *unless* one has fallen into financial difficulty.

The Rabbi as Philanthropic Advisor

Ellen Flax

> *May my lot be with those who collect charity, but not with those who distribute charity.*
> —BT *Shabbat* 118b

As hard as it may be to believe, giving away money—especially when it is not your own money—can be a difficult task. Thanks to an explosive growth in the number, and wealth, of foundations over the past decade and a half, a small but influential group of rabbis have had the privilege of serving as philanthropic advisors to family foundations that support and often help shape the priorities of the Jewish community. These rabbis/philanthropic advisors have learned first hand about the joys, as well as the challenges, that are associated with this little understood line of work.[1]

The Growth of Family Foundations

Between 1997, the year of my ordination, and 2007, foundation assets in the United States more than doubled, from $330 billion to $670 billion. During the same time period, foundation grant making nearly tripled, from $16 billion in 1997 to $43 billion in 2007.[2] Much of this growth was fueled by the dramatic increase in the number and economic strength of family foundations—charities that feature strong donor or donor-family involvement. It is estimated that two-thirds of the nearly 38,000 family foundations in the United States were established after 1990; 27 percent since 2000 alone. These charities control assets that total nearly $270 billion and make grants that exceed $16 billion annually.[3] This one-to-two-

---

ELLEN FLAX (NY97) is the rabbi of the Village Nursing Home and directs the Schusterman Rabbinical Fellowship program in New York, New York; she is also a consultant to foundations and nonprofit organizations.

decade-long growth in philanthropy, experts in the field predict, is but a harbinger of even more charitable activity in the coming decades, as the Baby Boom generation is poised to inherit at least $41 billion by 2052.[4] (Although the Great Recession has had a significant impact on the figures cited above—as of this writing, portfolios and foundation assets are still 20 to 30 percent lower than where they were as of September 2008—there are nonetheless truly substantial sums of money available, or potentially available, for charitable giving.)

Assessing the Jewish slice of the total philanthropic pie is a challenge, since there is no accepted definition of a Jewish foundation.[5] Pre-recession, the Jewish Funders Network (JFN) estimated that Jewish family and independent foundations controlled $30 billion in assets. As of 2003, some estimated that there were as many as 10,000 Jewish family foundations; however, like the majority of family foundations in the United States, these entities are likely to be small (controlling less than $5 million in assets) and donating less than $100,000 annually.[6]

As the size of a foundation's assets increases, so is the likelihood that it will employ professionals to manage its grant making. According to the Foundation Center, 27 percent of family foundations with assets that exceed $5 million employ paid workers. Similarly, as the assets of Jewish foundations have grown over the past decade, these Jewish charities, too, appear to have hired professional staff. In 2005, for example, JFN established a Foundation Professionals initiative to provide programming and support to the burgeoning number of foundation workers serving in its member organizations, since approximately one-third now have paid staff.[7]

In the Jewish sector, family foundation staff hail from a wide variety of professional backgrounds, including lawyers, social workers, educators, former federation officials, and businessmen and women. Not surprisingly, some of these staffers have been rabbis. Since the beginning of the family foundation boom, approximately a dozen colleagues from all denominations have helped direct the grant making for charities established by many of the foremost names in North American Jewish philanthropy, including: S. Daniel Abraham, Charles Bronfman, Edgar Bronfman, the Crown family, the Cummings family, Charles and Lynn Schusterman, Michael Steinhardt, and Leslie Wexner.[8]

THE RABBI AS PHILANTHROPIC ADVISOR

The Pleasures—and Challenges— of Being a Foundation Professional

Like many other colleagues (rabbinic and laypeople) who do or did this work, I fell into it by happenstance. Having worked as a journalist before entering rabbinical school, I relied on my writing and research skills to support my studies, in addition to the usual array of student pulpits and religious-school positions. Before long, I was crafting grant proposals, writing reports on grant-funded projects, and providing technical assistance to a couple of nonprofits, all critical experiences that would help me later in my work at foundations. But it wasn't until I heard Rabbi Rachel Cowan, then the director of the Jewish Life and Values Program at the Nathan Cummings Foundation, address my class at HUC about noncongregational options for rabbis, that a little light bulb went on in my head: that foundation work was something that I would probably really enjoy doing and was likely qualified to do, given my skills and background.

Several foundations (as both an employee and consultant) later, I feel I have been truly privileged to have served in these settings. With the backing of some extraordinarily generous families, I've been able to help shape programs that impact rabbinical education for Reform and Conservative students, expand informal education opportunities for Jews of all ages and denominations, and bolster the Jewish educational content of summer camps. Because I have worked for funders who are deeply invested in the wider community, I have also been able to work with organizations that improve formal and informal educational programs for low-income youth, maintain critical services for the poor and elderly, and expand arts and cultural offerings in underserved neighborhoods. As someone committed to *tikkun olam* (repairing the world) and strengthening both the Jewish and secular communities, I could not have asked for a better forum for pursuing so many of my interests and passions.

In retrospect, however, I realize that I was not nearly as prepared to do this work as I had initially thought I was. In talking to fellow travelers, both rabbis and laypeople, I learned that there was a significant learning curve for many of us, because working for a family foundation, especially a Jewish family foundation, is a world unto itself. Because each foundation's operations frequently reflect not only the priorities, but the personal preferences, of the founder/donor, many of the lessons learned at one job placement do not neatly transfer to another. Further, because this is such a new profession, training, ongoing career development, and professional standards could be more robust.[9]

Many of the challenges of this work also stem from the complicated relationship between money and power in our society. As has been noted elsewhere, once someone becomes a paid representative of a foundation or philanthropist, they are often treated differently by others.[10] From my own experience, I can reasonably surmise that some sought out my advice, returned my phone calls/emails with greater alacrity, and invited me to certain programs and events that I would not normally have had access to, once they learned about my affiliation with a particular foundation or philanthropist. Further, it was not unusual for acquaintances to approach me, unsolicited, to promote a grant proposal or to pitch the merits of their organization.

It was also a challenge learning how to say "no," firmly, clearly, and politely. As a rabbi, my natural inclination is to try to please and foster win-win situations. However, soon after starting this work, I realized that grant seekers would interpret anything positive I might have said about their organization or the soundness of their proposal/project as a solid "yes" (or at the very least, a strong "maybe") when I merely was trying to be friendly, helpful, or polite. Conversely, it was frustrating when potential applicants did not want to believe me when I told them, straight out, that the foundation was not interested in supporting their particular organization, project, or cause, and thus it did not make sense for them to pen a full proposal. From my vantage point, I felt my honesty could help them avoid needless work, but some viewed my naysaying as an invitation to redouble their efforts (which invariably resulted in a formal rejection). Consequently, I would often question myself and replay many conversations in my mind, to determine what—if anything—I might have said that could have been interpreted as encouraging.

Probably the greatest challenge of this work, at least for me, was shouldering the moral burden of stewarding someone *else's* funds—making me responsible for ensuring that (1) the money was spent on projects that reflected the vision and wishes of the foundation/philanthropist and (2) the funds were allocated as wisely and efficiently as possible. The various ethical choices I have to make with respect to spending and donating my own money are difficult enough—but being responsible for another person's or a foundation's funds, especially when the sums involved can make a real difference to an organization or the Jewish community as whole, was a totally different matter! I was grateful that the foundations I worked for established (or wanted me to help them fashion) guidelines, areas of interest, and priorities, which provided a strong framework for our giving and an assurance that our grant making was aligned with the donor's wishes. To ensure that our philanthropy was effective, I became very interested in evaluation methods, and I created reporting systems whereby the grantee and the foundation were in sync about the expected outcomes of any given grant—before any money changed hands.

What Rabbis Offer Foundations

My s'michah (rabbinical ordination), in the main, has been a blessing in this field. While I doubt I was ever hired specifically because I was a rabbi—indeed, I am sure that my background in general nonprofit and foundation work weighed far more heavily in the hiring decision—the fact that I came in with particular knowledge about the Jewish community, Jewish texts, and Israel and was presumed to possess traits associated with clergy (such as honesty and trustworthiness) was seen as a plus. While I was never tapped to be a particular philanthropist's "rabbi," I have led text study sessions, answered halachic (Jewish legal) questions, and have been asked to couch giving programs in Jewish terms as part of my responsibilities. Far more important, I've had to draw upon rabbinic skills, such as careful listening and counseling skills, to better understand the philanthropist's motivations for giving and the role that Judaism and Jewish identity play (both positively and negatively) in their lives and their charitable efforts.

To discover whether my experiences were typical or atypical, and to learn more about some of the joys and challenges experienced by other rabbis who direct grant making at family foundations, I surveyed all the colleagues I could identify in the field about their current or former experiences as a foundation professional.[11]

All but one of the colleagues I queried felt that their s'michah played at least somewhat of a role in the decision of the philanthropist or the family to hire them, while all noted that their prior work experience in the Jewish community likely played a more decisive role. One-third reported that the foundation indicated during the hiring process—either explicitly or implicitly—that it expected them to serve as the rabbi/spiritual advisor to the philanthropist, family, or board members. Significantly, twice as many—two-thirds—said they wound up taking on such a role once on the job. Typical tasks, at least initially, included leading Torah study or providing spiritual advice in a time of crisis. However, several were subsequently expected to serve as a service leader/spiritual leader of the philanthropist's congregation in addition to their regular job duties, which sometimes was a source of stress for the rabbi (who did not envision taking on this duty when she or he was hired) and/or for different family members, who were not necessarily of one mind about the rabbi assuming this role.

Not surprisingly, colleagues said that they drew upon many rabbinic skills on the job. These included: counseling, teaching, drawing upon knowledge of Israel, the Jewish community and Jewish texts, empathetic reflecting, espousing Jewish values, and public speaking. "While I was the executive director of a large foundation, I was more accurately the confidant and advisor of a philanthropist," said a colleague. "In that capacity, I used all of the people skills—listening, facilitating, discussing, challenging, hand-holding, teaching, caring—that I learned from my father and teachers."

While almost every rabbi reported that their *s'michah* made them and the ideas they espoused more credible in the eyes of their philanthropist/family/board, more than half said that their being a rabbi was also a source of tension at their foundation, making them a flashpoint for family or board members who had an uneasy connection to their Jewish identity. "The head of the family, for whom I worked and selected me without consultation with others, probably valued [my rabbinic] credential," said one colleague. "Others probably devalued the credential."

"I am not persuaded that being a rabbi is in itself an advantage or disadvantage [for doing this work,]" said another colleague. "Knowledge, experience, insights, and personality matter more. Given the ambivalence the community has towards rabbis, it is probably an advantage and disadvantage at the same time." Despite the challenges, colleagues reported, in the main, that foundation work was a highly rewarding way to express one's rabbinate—and if not one's rabbinate, as a way to express one's deepest values.

"As a rabbi, I wanted to teach, counsel and help people, work to build Jewish community, connect people to God, assure the future of Jewry," said a colleague. "Philanthropic work gave me the chance to work in all these areas. I considered this as legitimate an area of rabbinic work (and as positive expression of being a rabbi) as would have been a synagogue or more formal religious/rabbinical setting. As many Jews do not come to synagogue—or put up their guard against a formally religious approach, I considered the philanthropic setting to be an especially fruitful setting for rabbinic work. Finally, as a rabbi I wanted to cross denominational lines and connect Jews to each other. The foundation was more open to K'lal Yisrael than a denominational synagogue."

"What makes a gift Jewish, and to what extent that gift expresses the giver's Jewish identity, are serious questions in our community today," said another colleague. "How those questions are answered can make a real impact on how anyone gives. Take that impact to the level of six, seven, and eight figures and it can be felt by the community (either positively or negatively) for generations. If the rabbi's primary role is as a teacher, then working with philanthropists helps ensure that they will make their giving decisions from a Jewishly grounded place regardless of where they choose to make their gifts."

"This work is my rabbinate," said a third rabbi. "It really bothers me when people say, 'So you used to be a rabbi' or even 'So you used to practice as a rabbi.' This is 100 percent my rabbinate. This is the current manifestation of how I am serving as a Jewish leader seeking to make meaningful change in the Jewish community and the world."

Jewish Values for the Rabbi as Philanthropic Advisor

As noted above, rabbis who work as philanthropic advisors, like their lay and secular colleagues, face a range of challenges with respect to how they interact with both grant seekers and the families/donors that they serve—challenges that can wear down and potentially distort even those with a healthy, balanced sense of self. Nonprofits often accord us respect, attention, and special treatment that we don't necessarily deserve, ego strokes that make it easy to forget about the inherit power imbalance between those who seek funds and those who give funds away. At the same time, a good philanthropic advisor has to sublimate his or her own ego—and in some cases, strong opinions about the best use of limited funds—to ensure that the donor's vision is fulfilled.

Fortunately, Jewish values and wisdom can help the philanthropic advisor, including the rabbi/philanthropic advisor, navigate these tensions. Some of the values that I have used to frame my work—to imbue it with a sense of *k'dushah* (sanctity)—include:

Anavah (Humility)—never giving the impression (or falsely believing) that I have power that I do not have;

Derech Eretz (Decency)—treating all grant seekers with respect, since they are doing the really hard work of repairing the world;

Emunah (Trustworthiness)—always behaving and speaking in such a way that I am worthy of the trust that both the foundation/donor and the nonprofits place in me;

Hochmah (Wisdom)—keeping abreast of the latest trends and information in the field, so I can wholeheartedly say that a particular organization or program should receive funding;

Rachamim (Compassion)—having reasonable expectations for all the grantee organizations—and co-workers—with which and whom I work; and

Yetzer HaTov (A Good Inclination)—affirming that a foundation or donor's efforts, even if I do not agree with every funding decision, are for the general good of the community.

Most of all, I try to keep in mind the words of that ancient Jewish commentator on philanthropy, Rabbi Yose, who taught in *Pirkei Avot* 2:12: "Let your friend's money be as dear to you as your own." By drawing upon rabbinic skills and Jewish values and teachings, I hope I am living up to that admonition.

Notes

1. While a growing number of rabbis are involved in the giving and/or spending side of philanthropy—indeed, colleagues work in the allocations departments of local federations, direct programs

funded by prominent philanthropists, and serve as volunteer board members of foundations created by *tzedakah*-minded congregants and community members—this article will focus on the unique experiences of rabbis who serve/have served as grant-making staff and paid advisors to family foundations and wealthy individuals.

2. Steven Gunderson, "Current Trends in Philanthropy," *Journal of Jewish Communal Service* 84, no.1/2 (Winter/Spring 2009): 91–92.

3. Foundation Center, "Key Facts on Family Foundations," Revised Edition (April 2008).

4. John J. Havens and Paul G. Schervish, "Why the $41 Trillion Wealth Transfer Estimate Is Still Valid: A Review of Challenges and Questions," *The Journal of Gift Planning* 7, no.1 (January 2003): 11–15, 47–50.

5. Jeffrey Solomon, in "Jewish Foundations," *Journal of Jewish Communal Service* 81, no. 1/2 (Fall/Winter 2005): 101, notes: "Because there are serious definitional problems in creating a taxonomy for Jewish foundations, there is a paucity of reliable data as to numbers, dollar values and impact of these foundations. Among these issues are those having to do with the definition of a Jewish foundation. Is it a foundation whose principal is/was Jewish? Whose board is primarily Jewish? Whose historic giving patterns were primarily to the Jewish community? Exclusively? Somewhat? Must its charter specify a Jewish purpose? Is a foundation Jewish if founded by a Jewish principal whose distributions throughout the first generation were for the benefit of Jewish causes but today is governed by the heirs who are no longer Jewish and who no longer support Jewish causes?"

6. Ibid., 101; Foundation Center, "Key Facts on Family Foundations." In the United States, foundations are required to "pay out" at least 5 percent of their investment assets each year. This "pay out" includes the dollar value of their grants, as well as overhead.

7. The author would like to thank the JFN, and in particular, Stefanie Rhodes, Director, Member Services and Foundation Professionals, for their help with this article.

8. This figure was derived from polling foundation professionals as well as professionals at the JFN, whose members predominately range from secular to centrist Orthodox. Given that the ultra-Orthodox philanthropic sector tends to operate separately from other Jewish philanthropy, rabbis who might serve in a grant-making capacity for these charities were not included in my tally.

9. In recent years, several organizations have created training and professional development offerings for foundation professionals, including the Ford Foundation's GrantCraft initiative; the aforementioned Foundation Professional's program at the JFN; The

Grantmaking School, a W.K. Kellogg Foundation-funded initiative at Grand Valley State University; and the Heyman Center for Philanthropy and Fundraising at New York University.
10. See Roy W. Menninger, "Foundation Work May be Hazardous to Your Mental Health: Some Occupational Dangers of Grant Making and Grant Receiving," Council on Foundations (1981); Gary A. Tobin, "Family Philanthropy's Mad Hatter," *Foundation News & Commentary* 45, no.1 (January/February 2004): 1–4; Stefanie Rhodes, "The Dynamic Role of the Family Foundation Professional," *Journal of Jewish Communal Service* 84, no. 1/2 (Winter/Spring 2009): 32–36.
11. Nine colleagues graciously agreed to answer my survey or talk to me about their experiences. Given the high premium this field places on discretion, all the participants were promised anonymity.

Ethical Priorities in Giving *Tzedakah*

Ruth Adar

It is a positive mitzvah to give *tzedakah* when one has the means in hand. And a person needs to be very careful about it, more than all the positive *mitzvot*, because it may be a matter of life and death for the recipient.[1]

The Torah and the Rabbis recognized that the deprivations and indignities of poverty destroy the bodies and souls of the poor. Their answer to poverty: *tzedakah*. As the quotation from the Tur warns, when one is attempting to assist a vulnerable population, there are ethical issues to consider when we observe the mitzvah of *tzedakah*.

The mitzvah of *tzedakah* is incumbent upon every Jew. This requirement is based on numerous verses of Torah. For example:

> When you reap the harvest of your land, you shall not reap all the way to the edges of your field, or gather the gleanings of your harvest. You shall not pick your vineyard bare, or gather the fallen fruit of your vineyard; you shall leave them for the poor and the stranger: I the Eternal am your God.[2]

> If your kin, being in straits, come under your authority, and are held by you as though resident aliens, let them live by your side. Do not exact advance or accrued interest, but fear your God. Let your kin live by your side as such. Do not lend your money at advance interest, nor give your food at accrued interest.[3]

> If however, there is a needy person among you, one of your kin in any of your settlements in the land that the Eternal your God is giving you, do not harden your heart and shut your hand against

---

RABBI RUTH ADAR (LA08) is the Visiting Assistant Rabbi at Congregation Ner Tamid in Henderson, NV, and a teacher at Lehrhaus Judaica in Berkeley, CA.

your needy kin. Rather, you must open you hand and lend whatever is sufficient to meet the need.[4]

Even in the best of times, *tzedakah* funds rarely outstrip the need for *tzedakah*. In difficult times like the present, every person wishing to fulfill the mitzvah of giving *tzedakah* will have to make choices about the allocation of funds: whom shall I assist, and whom shall I regretfully refuse? Moreover, for those who have lost jobs or who have close relatives in need, issues of *tzedakah* may be particularly painful, because they have little to give or have a responsibility to family members who are struggling.

Many Jews, when faced with questions about *tzedakah*, offer up two nuggets of learning on the subject: first, the word means "righteousness" or "justice," not charity; and second, that a loan or finding someone a job is "the highest form of giving." Both of these are true, and knowledge of them is laudable, but they are insufficient equipment for making the best decisions about *tzedakah*. They address the "why" and some of the "how" of giving, but they do not shed any light on the subject of who will be chosen as a recipient or how to choose an appropriate organization for *tzedakah*.

The tradition offers us guidance that can relieve some of the anxiety in making these decisions. Some guidance takes the form of halachah, and some the form of aggadah. In either case, the tradition guides but does not bind, due to the principle of *tovat hanaah*: the right of the individual giver to divide his *tzedakah* as he chooses among those entitled to receive.[5]

Historic Priorities Regarding Individuals

The Rambam's famous "ladder of *tzedakah*" in *Mat'not Aniyim* 10.17 provides some guidance on how to give by specifying the merit attached to various modes of giving. He describes eight levels (rungs) of giving, from the highest to the lowest:

1. Giving a person the means to independence via a partnership or loan.
2. Giving *tzedakah* anonymously to an unknown recipient.
3. Giving *tzedakah* anonymously to a known recipient.
4. Giving *tzedakah* publicly to an unknown recipient.
5. Giving *tzedakah* before being asked.
6. Giving adequately after being asked.

7. Giving willingly, but inadequately.
8. Giving unwillingly.[6]

The ladder offers guidance on how best to give, but it does not help with the problem of multiple worthy applicants, and that may be a very serious matter indeed, as the Baal HaTurim pointed out in this article's opening passage. Nor does it address the issue of choices in institutional *tzedakah*, where an individual may give to an organization that will take responsibility for the disbursement of money or services.

The Rambam specifies other, less well-known hierarchies of *tzedakah* in *Mat'not Aniyim* that can assist us in setting *tzedakah*-giving priorities in a time of limited resources. These appear in various places and must be pieced together to form a ladder of the sort he so conveniently describes in 10:7.

Pidyon sh'vuim, the ransom of captives, has the highest priority for *tzedakah* funds. According to the Rambam, "there is no greater commandment than the ransom of captives," and the Talmud, codes, and modern responsa are all in agreement with him.[7] The obligation is not limitless: in the time of the Mishnah, the Rabbis were aware that if Jews were willing to bankrupt themselves to pay exorbitant ransoms, it might well serve to encourage the kidnapping and imprisonment of Jews. In *Mishnah Gittin*, therefore, the Rabbis specify that for the welfare of society, captives should not be redeemed for "more than their monetary value."[8] The Gemara expands on the idea, pointing out that limitless ransom could bankrupt the society and encourage an industry of kidnappers.[9] Their concerns about such industries unfortunately remain relevant today. Some halachic authorities suggest that in our day, Jews who are in jail might also be considered "captives" in need of ransom.[10]

Most halachic sources are in agreement that after the ransom of captives, the first *tzedakah* obligation of an individual is to keep herself off the public dole. It is an acknowledgment that anyone can have a reversal of fortune and that the *tzedakah* resources in any community are limited. The codes are unequivocal on the subject, insisting that a person is obligated to give his own *parnasah* (sustenance) priority over that of any other person.[11] A person should not endanger her ability to live and earn a living by giving beyond her means. Moses Isserles made the point in the *Mapah*, his gloss on the *Shulchan Aruch*, when he referred to giving beyond one's means as *bizbuz* (a waste).[12]

After individual stability, the Rambam provides two sets of priorities that might be summarized as "near before far." The needs of close family members take priority over those of distant cousins.[13] This ladder of priorities may come as a relief to families whose resources are stretched thin by loss of income: Funds spent assisting relatives in need qualify as *tzedakah*. However, one should not expend an entire *tzedakah* budget on a single recipient.[14] Nor should *tzedakah* funds be spent for support of a needy parent if other funds are available, since honoring one's parent is a separate mitzvah.[15]

A servant in one's household takes priority over the poor nearby, who take priority over the poor far away.[16] The poor of the Land of Israel are the exception to the "near before far" principle. While they do not take precedence over ailing impoverished relatives or the poor in one's own city, their needs have priority over the needs of the poor in a distant city.

There are also strong traditions for the support of Torah scholars, Torah education, and the needy in the Land of Israel, the giving to any of which qualifies as *tzedakah*.[17] Other texts suggest priorities according to a prospective recipient's gender (women are deemed more vulnerable than men), intensity of need, or even level of education.[18]

The tradition also offers us an ordering of intensity and kinds of needs. A person whose life is threatened by starvation has priority over someone in need of clothing, which we learn from discussions about the questioning of petitioners for *tzedakah* funds. We are encouraged to question someone asking for clothing about her circumstances and eligibility, but a person asking for food should not be delayed by questioning, because his life or health may be at stake.[19]

In the context of *tzedakah*, "need" is not limited to the most minimal survival requirements: a person may give *tzedakah* so that another Jew may be able to fulfill ritual obligations, such as obtaining a mezuzah to put on the door or providing Torah education for children through school tuition or camp fees.

Issues to Consider When *Tzedakah* Is Given via an Institution

All of the ladders listed thus far have to do with *tzedakah* given to individuals. As in our own day, the community also had institutions for the gathering and distribution of *tzedakah*. In Rabbinic times, each community was assumed to have a communal food supply, the *tamchui*.[20] By the twelfth century, the Rambam could say that he had never seen nor heard of a Jewish community that did not have a *kupah*, a charity box, for *tzedakah*. The *tamchui* existed at that time in some communities and not in others.[21] Recipients need not be Jewish: the codes specify that everyone who asks for bread should be given food whether they are Jewish or not.[22]

In the present day, the *kupah* takes many forms: a rabbi's discretionary fund, a Federation fund for relief of the poor, or the Hebrew Free Loan Society,[23] among others. MAZON[24] is one example of a *tamchui*; however, given that recipients may be Jewish or non-Jewish, any community food bank or kitchen would qualify as a *tamchui* for the purpose of giving *tzedakah*, provided that its administration met the standards we would expect of a Jewish agency carrying out the same mitzvah.

Prudence and honesty in management of *tzedakah* funds is a serious matter. The Rabbis honor those who encourage others to give.[25] Nearby that passage, however, they cite tannaitic sayings that regulate *gabba-ei tzedakah* (administrators of *tzedakah*): they must work in pairs and must not separate; they may not put coins in their pockets; they may not make change for themselves; and they must count coins one by one. If collecting for the *tamchui*, they may sell excess food donations, but they may not purchase any of it for themselves.[26]

The Rabbis recognized that *tzedakah* funds may be a temptation and that the judgment of even the best-intentioned fundraiser may be clouded by the sums involved. They worried that there are myriad ways by which one might take personal advantage from control of those resources. Just like moderns, they were concerned that institutions be well run.

New Ideas about *Tzedakah* Institutions

These concerns, which are still with us today, form the basis of an ongoing conversation in philanthropic and communal service circles as administrators and donors consider what it is to be a well-run *tzedakah* organization. Since the mid-1990s, there has been a discussion of the limitations of philanthropy and charitable giving as it has developed in the United States. Eric Thurman, an expert in international philanthropy, has coined the term "performance philanthropy," referring to a kind of philanthropy that is less concerned with receipts (from donors) and more concerned with results in the form of life-change for the recipients. He argues that most donors are attuned to the problems of fraud and theft, but that the real problems faced by many agencies today are waste and the basic effectiveness of the gift in making genuine change.[27] Other voices in the same discussion talk about "venture philanthropy," using the model of venture capitalism, with resources and funding "invested" in a charity in search of a social return on investment.[28]

While most of this discussion has taken place among foundations and major philanthropists, this sort of innovation in thinking about giving has also made for changes in the choices available to small donors. For instance, the online nonprofit kiva.org serves as a network for aspiring micro-lenders all over the world and applicants for microloans in the developing world. The minimum loan is $25. As of January 15, 2008, 226,575 small lenders had made $19,673,010 in loans to the working poor of the third world via kiva.org.[29] Kiva.org and similar organizations have inspired projects such as the Jerusalem Interest Free Microfinance Fund (JIMF), which acts to make training and interest-free loans available to Jerusalem's poor, in compliance with both Jewish and Islamic law.[30] More recently, Jewish Funds for Justice initiated 8th Degree, a project using microlending to help rebuild small businesses in New Orleans.[31]

Younger potential givers of *tzedakah* have a different set of expectations than did their parents, stemming both from the new thinking about philanthropy and from the growth of innovative nonprofits. These new trends need to be examined in light of the halachah and the tradition, with an eye to melding the best of each. A 2006 article in the *New York Jewish Week* indicates that these discussions among Jews are yet to take place.[32]

A nineteenth century responsum by Rabbi Esriel Hildesheimer, an Orthodox rabbi and respected *posek* (one who gives a ruling on matters of Jewish law) in Germany offers a model for some of what will be needed in a discussion about philanthropic methods and philosophies. After Emancipation, the old Jewish communities that had been semiautonomous began to reorganize as voluntaristic communities. One of the issues facing them was that old modes of fundraising simply could not work: Jews were citizens of the larger society, and the Jewish courts no longer had any way to enforce giving to communal funds. Since there were still Jewish institutions in need of funding, how was that to take place? It was common practice in the non-Jewish communities of Europe to publish lists of donors with the amounts they had given, as an incentive for donors to give or give more. In 1867, a German Jewish organization adopted this practice, publishing the names and amounts in the *Israelit*, a German-language Orthodox periodical.

Rabbi Eleasar Ottensosser, who had established a small Talmud school in Bavaria, was concerned by this practice, which seemed to him to violate the halachah. He raised the issue with Rabbi Seligman Baer Bamberger, a leading Talmudist of the time. Rabbi Bamberger would not rule on the matter unless two other leading Talmudists, Rabbi Jakob Ettlinger and Rabbi Hildesheimer, ruled in concert with him. In other words, he saw this matter as having such serious repercussions that he was unwilling to rule alone. On the one hand, anonymity in giving has a high value, and Rabbi Ottensosser and others understood it to have the force of a command. On the other hand, the publicity was deemed necessary in order to raise sufficient funds to keep the schools of Torah open. Ultimately Rabbi Hildesheimer ruled leniently, allowing the practice of publishing donor lists, which set a precedent that stands to this day throughout the modern Jewish world.[33]

New ideas about philanthropy require similar cooperative study in light of the tradition before simply adopting them as *tzedakah* practice. For instance, much of the new philanthropy has at its core a belief that a high degree of donor control is a key element of responsible giving. This is a sharp contrast to the emphasis on release of control embodied in the ancient practices of *tzedakah* such as *pei-ah*, in which the farmer simply walks away from the corners of his field, leaving them for the poor to harvest. The Maimonidean ladder of *tzedakah* in chapter 10 of *Mat'not Aniyim* similarly puts a high premium on anonymity of giving and on the empowerment of the needy. For now, it behooves every Jew to take care that the institutions to which he gives scarce *tzedakah* funds adhere to standards at least as high as his own.

There is also aggadic material concerning *tzedakah* and the values that inform it. In *K'tubot* 67b there is a series of stories about extravagance and *tzedakah*. In one, a man applies to Rava for "fat chicken and old wine." Rava asks if he has considered the burden of expense that will put on the community. Just as this discussion takes place, Rava's sister appears with a bountiful meal of fat chicken and old wine. Rava, properly embarrassed, apologizes to the man for not being willing to feed him as well as Rava feeds himself and invites him to share the meal. The story holds up several values simultaneously: it is legitimate for Rava to inquire about the burden of an extravagant request, but it is not appropriate for him to ask that question while munching on delicacies he is unwilling to share.

Another narrative: Rabbi Eleazar was a custodian of *tzedakah*. He came home one day and asked his family what *tzedakah* had been given out during his absence. They replied that several people came, and they received the food and then offered prayers for Eleazar. He replies, cryptically, that this is not the proper response. Later, other people come to the house while he is out, are given food, and revile his name. Eleazar says that that is the proper response.[34]

This is a more difficult story: why would Rabbi Eleazar say that harsh words were the proper response to receiving the *tzedakah* in his house? Eleazar is not present in person; in both cases, the *tzedakah* has become an impersonal transaction. It lacks a face-to-face quality. He is at a distance from the poor, communicating with them through servants or his wife. They receive only the food, which is better than no food, but they have no direct contact with Eleazar. The comfort and Torah that might have come with the food are absent. From this we may learn several values: that the "personal touch" has value, that food alone is not sufficient, and that a *tzedakah* administrator who is "too important" or "too busy" to connect with his clients is not doing the best possible job. Eleazar may have been suggesting that his administration lacked *anavah*, humility.

This story also challenges our expectations of gratitude from the recipients of *tzedakah*. *Derech eretz* (good manners) might require the recipient of *tzedakah* to express thanks to the donor, but it is inappropriate to make *tzedakah* decisions on the basis of one's expectations of gratitude from the recipient.

Finally, the words of the prophets on this subject are urgent in the extreme: Care for the poor takes precedence over sacrifices and ritual requirements, and neglect of the poor is a breach of the covenant.[35] Relief of the poor is an urgent matter; it should be carried out without delay.

Summary

Certainly it is possible to fulfill the letter of the law of *tzedakah* by setting aside cash and then giving it away to at least two people or organizations. Doing so carelessly, however, carries the possibility of doing harm rather than good. In giving *tzedakah*, the ethical Jew will want to consider to whom the funds will be given, and how that giving will be carried out. If the recipients are organizations that will be acting as agents of the donor, they should be well run and treat their clients with the same respect required of an individual donor. If the recipients are individuals, then great care should be taken to make matters better, not worse, for those people, and to treat them with the respect due a fellow child of God.

Moving through the process of *tzedakah* with care for the ethical issues involved will move the world one step closer to the vision of a world redeemed, of a community in which no one is in need.

> Give readily and have no regrets when you do so, for in return the Eternal your God will bless you in all your efforts and in all your undertakings.[36]

Notes

1. Arba'ah Turim, *Yoreh Dei-ah, Hilchot Tzedakah*, 247.
2. Lev. 19:9–10.
3. Lev. 25:35–37.
4. Deut. 15:7–8.
5. Cyril Domb, ed., *Ma'aser Kesafim: On Giving a Tenth to Charity* (New York: Feldheim, Inc., 1980), 105.
6. *Mishneh Torah, Mat'not Aniyim* 10:7.
7. Ibid., 8:10; see also BT *Bava Batra* 8b; *Shulchan Aruch, Yoreh Dei-ah* 252; W. Gunther Plaut and Mark Washofsky, *Teshuvot for the Nineties* (New York: CCAR Press, 1997), 321, 322.
8. *Mishnah Gittin* 4.6.
9. BT *Gittin* 45a.
10. Moshe Feinstein quoted in Domb, *Ma'aser Kesafim*, 25. If a Jew is justly imprisoned for a crime of which he has been convicted in court, surely he does not qualify as a recipient of *tzedakah*.

"Captivity" is an interesting concept for further study: Are persons with an addiction "captives" that might be "ransomed"? What other situations might a Jew fall into and be considered a captive?

11. Arba'ah Turim, *Yoreh Dei-ah*, 251, cited in Domb, *Ma'aser Kesafim: On Giving a Tenth to Charity*, 38; see also *Mishneh Torah, Arachim VeCharamim* 8.13.
12. *Shulchan Aruch, Yoreh Dei-ah* 249.1.
13. *Shulchan Aruch, Yoreh Dei-ah* 7:13.
14. *Shulchan Aruch, Yoreh Dei-ah* 257.9.
15. *Aruch HaShulchan* 251.8.
16. *Mat'not Aniyim* 7.13, 8.10.
17. E.g., *Pesikta de Rav Kahana* 10.1.
18. Tzedakah, Inc., "To Whom To Give," http://www.just-tzedakah.org/guidelinesWhom.asp (accessed 13 August 13, 2007).
19. *Aruch HaShulchan* 251.12.
20. Literally, a communal soup pot. For an example, see BT *Shabbat* 118a.
21. *Mat'not Aniyim* 9.3.
22. *Shulchan Aruch, Yoreh Dei-ah* 251.13. The reason given was *darchei shalom*, the ways of peace.
23. http://www.hfls.org.
24. http://www.mazon.org.
25. BT *Bava Batra* 9b.
26. BT *Bava Batra* 8b.
27. Eric Thurman, "Performance Philanthropy," *Harvard International Review* 28, no. 104 (Spring 2006): 18–21.
28. Paul Brest, "In Defense of Strategic Philanthropy," *Proceedings of the American Philosophical Society* 149, no. 2 (June 2005): 132–40.
29. http://www.kiva.org/about/facts (accessed January 16, 2008).
30. http://jerusalemmicrofinance.com.
31. http://jewishjustice.org/jfsj.php?page=2.13.
32. Debra Nussbaum Cohen, "Generation Gap in Giving," *The New York Jewish Week* 219, no. 20 (October 6, 2006): 44–45, 52.
33. David Ellenson, "Tzedakah and Fundraising: A 19th Century Response," *Judaism* 45, no. 4 (Fall 1996): 490–97.
34. JT *Pei-ah* 21a.
35. E.g., Isa. 1:11–19.
36. Deut. 15:10.

The Biblical Debtor's Release (Deuteronomy 15:1–3): Bankruptcy It Isn't—Or Is It?

Robin Nafshi

It is not uncommon in the lay community to assume that the Bible was tolerant of bankruptcy. This is a common misread of Deuteronomy 15:1–3.[1] Most biblical commentators have concluded that Deuteronomy 15:1–3 actually has little to do with bankruptcy—a court procedure in which people who are unable to pay their debts get protection from their creditors and, more importantly, get their debts wiped out. Deuteronomy 15:1–3 reads:

מִקֵּץ שֶׁבַע־שָׁנִים תַּעֲשֶׂה שְׁמִטָּה: וְזֶה דְּבַר הַשְּׁמִטָּה שָׁמוֹט כָּל־בַּעַל מַשֵּׁה יָדוֹ אֲשֶׁר יַשֶּׁה בְּרֵעֵהוּ לֹא־יִגֹּשׂ אֶת־רֵעֵהוּ וְאֶת־אָחִיו כִּי־קָרָא שְׁמִטָּה לַייָ: אֶת־הַנָּכְרִי תִּגֹּשׂ וַאֲשֶׁר יִהְיֶה לְךָ אֶת־אָחִיךָ תַּשְׁמֵט יָדֶךָ.

(1) Every seventh year you shall make a release. (2) This will be the matter of the release of the debt: every creditor shall remit [literally, forget his hand on] the due that he claims from his fellow; he shall not dun his fellow or his kinsman, for the proclamation is a release to the Eternal. (3) You may dun the foreigner, but your kinsman you must remit.

Rashi (eleventh century, France) asserts the following:

מקץ שבע שנים. יכל שבע שנים לכל מלוה ומלוה, תלמוד לומר קרבה שנת השבע, ואם אתה אומר שבע שנים (לכל מלוה ומלוה), להלואות כל אחד ואחד, האיך היא קרבה? הא למדת שבע שנים

ROBIN NAFSHI (NY05) serves as associate rabbi at Temple Beth-El in Hillsborough, New Jersey, and as the community rabbi and chaplain for Ohr Tikvah Jewish Healing Center of Jewish Family Service of Somerset, Hunterdon, and Warren Counties, New Jersey. She graduated from Cornell Law school in the mid-1980s.

למנין השמטה. **שמוט כל בעל משה ידו.** שמוט את ידו של כל בעל משה.

Every seventh year. One could think that this means at the end of seven years for each and every loan, for Torah says, the seventh year is approaching, and if you say seven years for each and every loan, how do you know the seven years are coming? So instead, you count seven years for the release. **All creditors release what is due.** The release of what is due shall be of all creditors.

Rashi's reading of the text is an excellent example of his *p'shat* approach to biblical commentary. His insights are simple, based on the literal reading of the text (in verse 2 for example, he simply restates the verse, changing the word order), but they are also supported through justification and logical reasoning. Rashi points out that to release each loan at the end of that loan's seven-year period (a process that sounds like bankruptcy) would be difficult, if for no other reason than the calendar. How do you keep track of the seven years for each loan? Instead, he claims, the text means that every seven years, every creditor releases all debts. Rashi's grandson, the Rashbam (twelfth century, France), comments only on verse 2, and then only on one phrase within that verse. He writes:

כי קרא שמטה ליי. כלומר כי הגיע זמן שמיטה, כמו מקראי קודש (ויקרא כג:ב), קרא עלי מועד (איכה א:טו), קראו צום (ירמיה לו:ט) כולם לשון זמן.

For it is called a release to God. That is said because the time of the release approaches, like "a sacred occasion," (Leviticus 23:2) "a proclaimed fixed time," (Lamentations 1:15) and "a proclaimed fast," (Jeremiah 36:9)—all words of time.

The Rashbam, like his grandfather, uses a *p'shat* approach with the text. He is concerned only with the phrase "it shall be a release to God." While other commentators compared that phrase to other releases to God (more on this later), the Rashbam doesn't. His *p'shat* is of a different nature. He heightens the sanctification of the release, comparing it to other sacred occasions delineated in *Tanach*. The Rashbam wrote at a time when Jews and Christians alike were engaging with the biblical text, and Christians often came to

Jews for lessons in Hebrew. It would have been easy to simply say one release to God is just like another release to God. The Rashbam, on the other hand, while looking at the plain meaning of the text, makes a more sophisticated analysis.

It is clear that he did not read Deuteronomy 15:1–2 as a release whose purpose was to benefit an overwhelmed debtor. Every seven years, each member of the community was to refrain from collecting the debts owed to him. This release is like other seven-year releases, such as the release of slaves and the laying fallow of the land. Later, both the Ramban (thirteenth century, Spain) and the Sforno (sixteenth century, Italy), agree. They state that the release in Deuteronomy comes from the release proclaimed by God in Exodus 23:11, when God commands, "the seventh year you shall rest the land and let it lie fallow."

Along these same lines, Abarbanel (fifteenth century, Portugal) conjures up a beautiful image:

ולכן אמר שתהיה השמטה כן שבת לה׳. ואמר גם כן שבת שבתון יהיה לארץ שהוא מאמר כולל. האמנם פרט שם שמטה קרקעות ולכן לא הוצרך לבאר אותה כאן כי אם שמטה כספים שלא התבארה שמה.

> Thus, he said, it will be like the Shabbat/rest to God. He said also it will be a complete rest for the land, and will be in the category of complete. The River Amunam splits there, releasing the earth, therefore, there is no need to break it forth now, for the release of money does not break forth there.

Yitzchak Arama (fifteenth century, Spain; expelled in 1492, and died just two years later) agrees that the release is to God. He then observes that the release of debts is one of four acts that runs counter to a person's nature. The four acts are found in *Parashat R'eih*. In the first (Deut. 14:22–27), one must set aside one-tenth of a yield of crops each year as a tithe to God. Next (Deut. 14:28–29), every third year, one must give a full tithe for the Levite and the poor. Third (Deut.15:1–2) is the release of debts, and fourth (Deut. 15:7–8), requires that one give charity to the poor. Arama wrote:

וכאשר נתן סדר אכילת מעשר שני והפרשת מעשר עני בשנה השלישית וכול עניים, שכולם הם דברים שצריכים לימוד והרגל,

מפני שטבע האנשים מנגדתן בקצת, נעתק לעניין שהוא יותר מנוגד מזה, ואמר: מקץ שבע שנים תעשה שמיטה. והוא דבר קשה מאוד בעיני האדם שילווה מממונו לחבירו ושימתין לו עליו עידן עידנים, ואחר שיעבור עליו השמיטה לא יהיה לו בו רשות לשואלו. והנה כאשר הזהיר על זה העניין מהשמיטה נעתק אל דבר יותר זר ויותר קשה בטבע האנשים והוא שיתן ממנו תחילה על מנת ישוב אליו עוד.

The text proceeds in ascending order of difficulty. First, the various tithes, all of which are matters requiring practice and training, because man is naturally reluctant to part with his own. It then proceeds to something running more counter to man's nature than this, and states, "every seven years make a release." It is very difficult for man to lend his fellow money and then wait a long period, only to be precluded from asking for it back when the year of the release arrives. Then, after the *sh'mitah* regulation has been imparted, an even more difficult demand is made: that he give something away from the outset without any intention of getting it back.

Arama's Torah commentary reflects the condition of Spanish Jewry at the time, including the immense pressures on them to convert. It is no wonder that he sees the debtor release of Deuteronomy as a pressure on man, which is difficult for him to endure. Arama chose the unusual title of *Akeidat Yitzchak* for his work to show that he had been bound by God to create it.

Ibn Ezra (twelfth century, Spain) compares this release for God to Shabbat, noting that Shabbat is for God. At the end of his commentary on verse 2, he writes:

שמטה לה׳. לכבוד השם שנתן לו הממון. וטעם הסמך המלה לשם, בעבור שבת היא לה׳.

A release to God. It is for the glory of God that he gives him money. This is explained by the *samekh* of the word for its own sake. [This has been the case because since the times] in the past, Shabbat is for God.

Ibn Ezra does raise the possibility that the release is not only for God. He seems to imply that the release is also to lessen the burden on the debtor, though, as is not surprising with a poet, philosopher, and well-traveled man like Ibn Ezra, his language is not always straight forward. Also regarding verse 2, he writes:

משה. במשקל מטה, והוא שם לפי דעתי. ולפי דעת הוא פועל. ובעל כמו והחכמה תחיה בעליה (קהלת ז:יב), את נפש בעליו יקח (משלי א:יט). והטעם, מי שהדבר ברשותו. ישה. פועל יוצא, והלוקח יקרא נושה בו. יגש. ילחץ, כמו וכל עצביכם תנגושו (ישעיה נח:ג). והנה נראה הנויין בפעלי העתיד מבעלי הנויין.

Release. Of the weight of the staff, according to my awareness and according to the heightened awareness of the worker. The owner (or creditor or master) is like one with wisdom who gives life to those who have it, but takes away the life of the owner (or creditor or master). And the examination, that is the matter of the one's authority. **Lent.** The worker goes out, and the creditor will call on him. **Press.** He will force on all your debts; he will exhort you. Here we see the *nun* in the future actions of the owner's *nun*.

Ibn Ezra expresses a degree of sympathy with the debtor not found in the commentaries of Rashi or the Rashbam. Yes, the release is for God, but ultimately, Ibn Ezra notes that God calls for the release because of the burden on those who cannot afford to repay their debts. Without the release, they would be pressed, exhorted, and perhaps even killed by their creditors.

Both Rashi and the Rashbam focus their comments on the meaning of release. Rashi simply assumes that the text means at the end of the seventh year. His concern, as explained above, is whether the seven years is a general release or a release for each specific debt. Given his conclusion that it is a general release because of the difficulty of counting the seven years for each debt, it is surprising that he does not address this other calendaring issue—when during the seventh year.

In addition to the meaning of release, the Ramban and Ibn Ezra concern themselves with the meaning of the seven years. Ibn Ezra concludes that the release came at the beginning of the year. He writes:

מקץ שבע שנים תעשה שמטה. בתחלית השנה, כאשר פירשתי. והעד הקהל את העם. ונדבקה זאת הפרשה בעבור שאמר כי

מעשר עני הוא ללוי ולגר וליתום ולאלמנה. אמר וכן דבר השמטה. והטעם כמו שמטוה (מלכים ב ט:לג), והניחוה ותפול.

Every seventh year you shall make a release. In the beginning of the year, as I have explained. This is during the gathering of the people. They held to this explanation in the past, as it is said, for this is the time the poor would tithe to the Levite, the stranger, the orphan, and the widow. He said, thus, this is the matter of the release. And the explanation is like push her down (II Kings 8:33), lie down, and fall.

Ibn Ezra claims that it is better that a debtor should get rid of his debts before he makes his beginning of the year tithes/pledges to the Levite, the stranger, the orphan, and the widow. Otherwise, he would make his tithes/pledges at the beginning of the year and then eliminate them during the general debtor release at the end of the year.

The Ramban disagrees. But rather than offering his typical commentary, using *sod* or aggadah, he seeks to beat the grammarian Ibn Ezra at his own game. He bases his commentary on multiple readings of the word *mikeitz*:

אבל כך אני אומר כי הקץ והסוף יאמרו בכתוב על אחרית כל דבר, ופעמים הם בו אחריו חוץ ממנו. ומקצה אחיו (בראשית מז:ב), מקצה בחוברת (שמות כו:ד), ומקצתם יעמדו לפני המלך (דניאל א:ה), מקצות כנפיו ועד קצות כנפיו (מלכים א ו:כד), כלם אחרית בדבר המחבר ממנו והוא בתוכו. קץ כל בשר בא לפני (בראשית ו:יג), ובא עד קצו ואין עוזר לו (דניאל יא:מה), בא הקץ (יחזקאל ז:ב), קץ בא (שם פסוק ו) כלם תכלית הדבר, והוא אחריו שנקצץ ונחתך.

But I say this: *keitz* and *soph* are used in Scripture to denote "the end" of any matter, but sometimes they are within that extremity and sometimes after it, outside of it. Thus: *umiktzei* (and from among) his brethren (Genesis 47:2), *mikatzeh* (that is outmost) in the set (Exodus 26:4), *umiktzatam* (that at the end) they might stand before the king (Daniel 1:5), *miktzot* (from the uttermost part) of the one wing unto *k'tzot* (the uttermost part) of the other (I Kings 6:24)—all these are expressions of an extremity which is attached to the thing itself and is contained within it. [But in the following expressions:] *keitz* (the end of) all flesh is come before Me (Genesis 6:13), and he shall come to *kitzo* (his end), and none shall help him (Daniel 11:45), *hakeitz* (the end) is come (Ezekiel 7:2), *keitz* (an end) has come (Ezekiel 7:6)—all signify "the end" of the matter mentioned but it signifies a later period, for it has been severed and separated.

Ramban asserts the following:

ועד דרך הפשט יראה לי לשון הכתוב כפשוטו הוא ברור ומתוקן,
כי קץ הוא סמף וכן תרגומו.

By way of the simple meaning of the Scripture it appears to me that the language of Scripture in its plain sense is clear and correct. *Keitz* means "end" and so is its translations [as rendered by Onkelos and Yonathan, who also translate: "at the end"].

and then concludes:

שהוא מדרש מפני שלא אמר השנה השביעית תעשה שמטה, ירמוז
כי בסוף השבע תעשה שמטה יותר מן ההתחלה. ורצונם בקץ הזה,
חוץ ממנו. ויכול אדם לתבוע חובו ביום האחרון של שנת השמטה
ולא תשמט עד הלילה, שכך מצינו בתוספתא (שביעית ח:יא)
שכותבין פרוזבול ערב ר"ה של מוצאי שביעית.

Because Scripture did not say "the seventh year you shall make" [but instead said *"mikeitz,"* seven years], it is more suggestive that you effect the remission at the end of the seven [years] than at the beginning. And the intent of [the Rabbis in using here] this term "end" is beyond it. Thus a creditor can demand his debt on the last day of the year of the release, and it is not remitted until the night, for thus we find in the Tosefta (Shevi'it 8:10) that they may write a prozbul (a declaration before a court by a creditor and signed by witnesses to the effect that the loan in question would not be cancelled by the law of release) on the day before the New Year of the outgoing seventh year.

Abarbanel and the Ramban seem to be in agreement that the release of the debts occurs at the end of the seventh year, not at the beginning. Abarbanel comments:

ורבי אברהם פירש מקץ שבע שנים מתחלת השבע שנים כי בידוע
שאחר שש השנים תהיה השנה השביעית שנה השמטה ולהיות הראש

והסוף קצות הדבר אומר על ההתחלה מקץ. והרמביי״ן זערונו לברכה פירש מקץ שהוא סוף השבע שנים שעברו. והיא השנה השביעית שנת השמטה כי הנה בעשרה האחד הוא ראש אותו מספר והעשירי הוא סופו ונכון הוא.

Rav Abraham explains that the end of seven years begins the seven year period because in knowing that after six years it will be the year of rest, the year of release, and to be the first and the last, that ends the matter, he says of the beginning and the end. And the Ramban of blessed memory explains *mikeitz* that it is the end of the seven years that are to come. It is the year of rest, the year of release,...at the end, and this is correct.

Turning to contemporary commentators, Michael Hudson draws parallels between the Israelites and the Babylonians during the Bronze Age (2400 B.C.E.–1400 B.C.E.).[2] He points to several edicts that declared debts canceled or released debt prisoners from captivity during this 1,000-year period. These edicts, he explains, usually correspond to religious new years, monarch transitions, or other nationwide festivals. He even explains that the word "Hallelujah" contains the ritual term "alulu," which was chanted by Babylonia debt slaves once they were freed and anointed with oil. According to Hudson, the Babylonian tradition was lost and then reintroduced among the Israelites. He writes:

> We do not have the original version of Deuteronomy as presented to Josiah, but only the post-exilic elaboration of the laws. In this final form they were once again subjected to nearly two centuries of Babylonian cultural influence by the Jewish community in exile. To call the septennial freeing of debt servants and the institution of the Jubilee year a "folk memory" is to dodge the issue of just how the practice survived and was modified into Jewish law. Josiah's anger that the old Deuteronomic laws had been abandoned suggests that the memory had lapsed. In such cases, practices must be reintroduced anew. In this case, the Deuteronomic laws were made public by royal edict, under the council of the Temple priesthood. This centralized policy-making nexus enabled the laws to be restarted in a new, theocratic context.[3]

Another contemporary writer, Rabbi Steven Resnicoff, a bankruptcy professor at DePaul University, adamantly asserts that the release has nothing to do with aiding a debtor in need. He claims that the obligation to repay a debt is an affirmative *mitzvah* and that the seven-year release was part of the overall renewal designed to remind people of the existence of God and of God's ownership of the world and everything in it. Debt cancellation reminds people of their transient nature.[4]

Despite Resnicoff's assertion, Ibn Ezra's sympathy toward debtors is echoed in modern times. There is a school of thought that Deuteronomy 15:1–3 is meant to benefit the poor. These sentiments suggest that we cannot ignore the related benefit for those who are overwhelmed by their debts, based on *Mishnah Sh'vi-it* 10:9, which states, "whoever repays a debt in the seventh year, the sages are well pleased with him."

Rabbi W. Gunther Plaut comments that the verses in Deuteronomy emphasize both personal holiness—remembering that we are children of God—and humanitarian concerns—that the children of God are responsible for one another.[5]

Finally, in the JPS Torah commentary, *Etz Hayim*, the editors write:

> The Torah here is concerned with the type of debt incurred by the poor and insolvent: a farmer in dire need of funds because of crop failure and a city dweller destitute as a result of unemployment. Loans to such individuals were regarded as acts of philanthropy rather than commercial ventures, and the forgiving of such loans was an extension of the generosity. The remission of debts and other provisions for the relief of debtors are part of the Torah's programs for preserving a balanced distribution of resources across society.

After the destruction of the Second Temple, the Rabbis extended the release of debts to countries other than Israel. Hillel, however, allowed lenders to get around the release through his enactment of a *prozbul*, a declaration made in court, before the execution of a loan, specifying that the release of debts not apply to the loan to be transacted. *Mishnah Sh'vi-it*, Chapter 10, specifically codifies Hillel's enactment.

The Jews of Spain in the thirteenth century did not observe the debtor's release, and the Jews of Germany made use of the *prozbul*. While the *Shulchan Aruch* mentions that the debtor's release was operative both in and out of Palestine, Moses Isserles adds that the majority of Jewish authorities in Germany were indifferent to or ignored the custom.[6]

The debtor's release does not apply in Israel today. The principal reasons relate to the fixed date of payment, the guaranty attached, and the terminology of present-day notes that abrogate the application.[7]

In general, liberal Diaspora Jews have not been concerned (other than perhaps as an intellectual exercise) with the meaning and application of the biblical debtor's jubilee. But we are concerned with the financial burdens placed on our brothers and sisters.

Research by the Federal Reserve indicates that household debt is at a record high relative to disposable income. Some analysts are concerned that this unprecedented level of debt might pose a risk to the financial health of U.S. households. For the calendar year 2008, over one million Americans filed for personal bankruptcy: more than 714,000 sought to wipe out their debts and nearly 360,000 sought the help of the court in restructuring their debt in order to repay their bills.

In our pastoral work, reaching out with compassion and care is first and foremost. Many of those Jews we encounter feel a sense of shame or embarrassment because of their financial woes—especially if they have had to turn to the bankruptcy court or a debt or credit counselor for assistance. To the extent that we can reassure them that helping an overwhelmed debtor out from under a mound of debt is as old as the Bible itself, we let them know that they are not alone, that people throughout history have sought similar help, and that our religious tradition affirms that giving an overburdened debtor the opportunity to wipe out debts is a deeply Jewish act.

Notes

1. For thirteen years before I entered rabbinical school, I worked as a legal author and editor with Nolo.com, specializing in debt, credit, and bankruptcy law. A few times when I was interviewed on Christian radio programs, I received calls from people in a state of panic about their debts. Often, their ministers had told them that they were obligated to repay their bills and that their religion prohibited them from acting otherwise. These were people so overwhelmed by their financial woes that they had no means of ever getting out of debt—unless they filed for bankruptcy. I frequently told them so, and then reassured them that bankruptcy had its origins in the Bible.

2. Michael Hudson, *The Lost Tradition of Biblical Debt Cancellations* (New York: Henry George School of Social Science, 1993).
3. Ibid., 42.
4. Steven Resnicoff, "Viewpoint: A Jewish Law Perspective on the Propriety of Discharging Personal Debts," *Bankruptcy Court Decisions: Weekly News and Comment,* February 3, 1998, Volume 40, Issue 5, A3–A4.
5. W. Gunther Plaut, ed., *The Torah: A Modern Commentary,* rev. ed (New York: URJ Press, 2005), 1257.
6. *Jewish Encyclopedia*, s.v. "Prosbul."
7. Ibid.

Money, Schism, and the Creation of American Reform Judaism

Dan Judson

"We usually do not look at religious activity through economic lenses," writes James Hudnot-Beumler in his economic history of the American Protestant church, "but occasionally we should, since when we do, we see some things in the history of religious life to which we are typically blind."[1] The history of American synagogues, similar to that of American churches, is rarely considered through economic lenses. Historians of Judaism typically focus on ideology, theology, and ritual, while issues related to money, such as dues, clergy salaries, and fundraising are generally neglected.[2] This article is a small corrective to that usual perspective and will examine the role of money in the founding of the first Jewish group in America dedicated to religious reform.

On November 24, 1824, forty-seven members of Congregation Beth Elohim in Charleston, South Carolina, submitted a memorial (petition) to the *Adjunta* (Board of Directors) calling for the synagogue to institute significant reforms in its worship practice. Charleston at this time vied with New York for the largest Jewish population in America, and Congregation Beth Elohim was a well-established synagogue, founded in 1749 as a traditional Sephardic congregation.[3] The Reform petition to the Board asked the Congregation for a number of changes including: services with English prayers, an English homily, and the elimination of superfluous prayers. Their petition was summarily rejected.[4] As a result of that rejection, the petitioners formed The Reformed Society of Israelites for Promoting True Principles of Judaism According to Its Purity and Spirit, the first group dedicated to reform in America. In 1826, the Society initiated a building campaign to build an alternative

---

RABBI DAN JUDSON (NY98) is the Director of Professional Development and Placement for the Hebrew College Rabbinical School. He is also a doctoral candidate in Jewish history at Brandeis University.

congregation in Charleston. It was unsuccessful in this endeavor, in part due to the changed economic climate of Charleston, but it worked within Beth Elohim to advocate changes. In 1840 the congregation effectively became Reform when it instituted several changes, including the addition of an organ. While scholars have looked extensively at the origins of the Reformed Society, what has almost entirely been ignored is the role of synagogue finances in its founding.[5] In the initial petition to the *Adjunta* of Beth Elohim, really the first Reform document in American history, roughly half of the petition is given over to the Reformers' extreme dismay over the way the synagogue was raising money by requiring people to pay for Torah honors.

Interestingly, 1824–1825 saw not just one, but two schisms in American synagogues in which the practice of selling Torah honors was at the center of controversy. Besides Charleston, Congregation Shearith Israel in New York, the oldest congregation in America, also had turmoil. A dispute over the practice of selling Torah honors brought long-simmering tensions in the congregation to the surface and led to the formation of an alternative synagogue, Congregation B'nai Jeshurun. As Jonathan Sarna argues, these two schisms were not simple congregational disputes; rather, they initiated a fundamental change in the structure of the Jewish community as American Judaism moved from "a synagogue-community" to a "community of synagogues." Prior to the 1820s each community had one synagogue that claimed authority over Jewish life. The 1820s saw two attempts in Charleston and New York—to overturn this model and break away from the established synagogue to create an alternative place of worship. Before the schisms, the synagogue had wielded monolithic authority with the power to compel obedience through fines and disciplinary action. Subsequent to these events, multiple and diverse synagogues arose in the same city, often competing with each other for the allegiance of individual Jews.[6]

While these schisms occurred in the same year, the goals of those seeking change were quite different. In Charleston, the focus was on religious reform. Inspired by reforms taking place both in the Charleston Protestant community as well as by the Jewish movement for reform in Germany, the Charleston Reformers sought significant liturgical changes. They repudiated the Rabbinic element in Judaism and sought a return to what they perceived as the pure biblical Judaism.[7] In New York, the group advocating for a schism sought a return to greater observance—what would be seen by today's standards as a move towards Modern Orthodoxy. But what both schisms had in common was that the breakaway groups were unhappy with the way the traditional synagogues were raising money by requiring people to pay for Torah honors.

For the Charleston Reformers, the practice of selling Torah honors raised two primary concerns. First, the part of the service in which such honors were solicited was conducted in Spanish. Thus, the practice conflicted with the goal of developing a modern English service. More importantly, however, the selling of Torah honors posed an ideological problem. The Reformers viewed the inclusion of money in religious services as incongruous with sacred worship. The trouble with bidding for honors in the middle of services may seem obvious to us now, but it was certainly not clear at the time, as evidenced by the large number of synagogues that utilized the practice. The Reformers' ideological objection reflected a new set of values regarding the role of money in synagogues. Their distaste for mixing money and services would become the standard Reform view, and it continues to have implications for how synagogues raise money today.

While the selling of Torah honors generated significant income for American synagogues in the early nineteenth century, the primary fundraising method employed by congregations during this period was the selling of seats. Synagogues sold seats permanently as well as rented them annually. In New York's B'nai Jeshurun congregation, for example, men's seats sold for $10 annually in 1830, while women's seats were auctioned. Shearith Israel had alternated between selling seats and levying an income tax, whereby each member of the synagogue would be assessed an annual fee. By 1805, however, the congregation had firmly decided against the income tax and placed a provision in its constitution prohibiting any income tax from ever being assessed on members.[8]

Voluntary contributions, including paying for Torah honors, provided an additional source of income. In their efforts to raise money this way, however, congregations in 1825 confronted the same problem that congregations face today, i.e., the inability to budget ahead of time exactly how much could be raised. Shearith Israel dealt with this problem by legislating a set amount to be donated for receiving an *aliyah*. In 1805, the board of trustees determined that the payment for an *aliyah* would be two shillings, and the money raised by these sales was to go towards its budget for communal *tzedakah*.[9] By setting an exact amount, the board ensured that the congregation would receive a stable source of income.

Although selling Torah honors, even by auctioning them, appears to have been ubiquitous in early American synagogues and occurred in most other parts of the Jewish world, there is almost no mention of this practice in Rabbinic literature. One of the earliest and most fascinating mentions of the custom comes from a responsa by the Maharik, Rabbi Joseph Colon (fifteenth century, Italy). A question comes to him regarding the practice of buying the first *aliyah* on Simchat Torah. The proceeds of this sale would go to paying for the synagogue lights. The potential problem with this was that the first *aliyah* of a Torah reading customarily goes to a *kohein*. The Maharik writes:

> ... [concerning] the custom of Ashkenazi and French synagogues in all of their communities that on *Shabbat Bereshit*[10] one of the community pays for the lights of the synagogue in order to be called up first to the Torah. The custom is for a *kohein* to pay for this mitzvah or he can release his honor and leave the shul. It once happened though that a *kohein* did not want to buy this *mitzvah* and also did not want to leave the synagogue, even to go to another synagogue that did not have this practice [of paying for the honor, thus the *kohein* could be given his *aliyah*].... The congregation agreed to bar him [the *kohein*] from the synagogue so that he will not enter the synagogue and they can follow the custom [of paying for the first *aliyah*]; by this the congregation will not diminish the honor of the Torah, nor the custom of our fathers. And so they did, and they compelled him ***by the city police*** to be out of the synagogue.[11]

The *t'shuvah* is interesting in many respects, not the least of which is the use of the gentile police force to remove the obstructionist *kohein* from the shul. It should also be noted in light of the congregational schism that is the focus of this article that paying for Torah honors often involves a conflict between tradition and the economic needs of the community and is associated with trouble and dissension.

The Maharik defends the custom of paying for the Torah honors with two arguments. First, paying for Torah honors is a way of giving homage to the Torah, and second, paying for Torah honors was a *minhag avoteinu*, a custom handed down through the generations. The Maharik repeatedly returns to the idea of paying for Torah honors being an old custom. It is unclear, though, when exactly this custom started and how it spread from Ashkenazi communities in Germany and France to the rest of the Jewish world.

Ismar Elbogen, in his history of Jewish liturgy, gives only cursory attention to the custom of paying for honors, pausing to say that it originated in the late Middle Ages and noting derisively, "Certainly, this paying for ritual functions was bound to lead to undesirable consequences, especially since for a time, they were even sold at public auction to the highest bidder."[12] He alludes to the problem of *aliyot* potentially going to the wealthiest individuals and not necessarily to the most respectable or pious. In his footnote to this section, he is even more condemnatory, saying flatly and without expansion that the practice of auctioning Torah honors "has nothing to do with Judaism."[13] Presumably he means that the practice was picked up from gentiles and does not comport with anything in Jewish tradition.

Despite Elbogen's contention that the practice isn't Jewish, there was some form of paying for honors in most American synagogues in the first half of the nineteenth century. At Mikveh Israel in Philadelphia, Isaac Leeser writes in 1842 of his desire to remove the practice, as it "interfere[s] with the solemnity of the service" and burdens regular worshipers over those who do not attend. He notes, "I would leave it to the good sense of the congregation to determine whether a mode of annual subscriptions could not be devised, which would effect a more equitable assessment."[14] The congregation heeded Leeser's plea and ended the practice a year later. Another example was Congregation Beth-El in Albany, where the practice of paying for Torah honors was tangentially associated with a rather unusual moment. In 1850, Isaac Mayer Wise was physically assaulted on the bimah by the president of the synagogue on Rosh HaShanah. The president had previously informed Wise that he was not to come to services. Wise's supporters, however, had bought the honor of removing the Torah for Wise, so he felt it was his right to come.[15] This incident is famous not only for the unusual spectacle of violence in the synagogue, but it would lead to the creation of Anshe Emeth, a synagogue in Albany where Wise's vision for Reform Judaism would prosper. The practice of paying for Torah honors is thus a small footnote in one of the defining moments of American Jewish history.

The custom's role in the creation of America's first group of Reform Jews, however, was more significant. The Charleston Reformers were primarily young, and some were politically active.[16] Many were also native-born and influenced by their Christian surroundings. "Like many Protestants of the day, the Charleston Reformers argued for changes that would, simultaneously, improve their faith and restore it to what they understood to be its original pristine form."[17] The Reformers' agenda is laid out in the memorial sent to the Board. It begins with dismay over the state of Jewish life: "[we] have witnessed with deep regret, the apathy and neglect which has been manifested towards our holy religion." The reasons for this apathy and neglect, according to the memorialists were "certain defects which are apparent in the system of worship, [which] are the sole causes of the evils complained of."[18] The petition then elucidates the evils and the proposed solutions. The first part of the proposed solutions relates to adding English to the service. The second part of the memorial focuses extensively on the practice of paying for honors.

The memorialists begin this section by saying that they will "set forth the entire uselessness and impropriety of this custom." The custom of Beth Elohim was to announce in Spanish the person who would be making the pledge for the honor and how much he would be giving, a custom that extended back to the initial founders of the synagogue who hewed to Sephardic traditions. By 1824 few members of the congregation spoke Spanish. The memorialists are outraged by the whole practice, but the use of Spanish just infuriates them more. They write:

> Besides the free scope which the practice of offering in a language understood by few affords to mischievous and designing men to pollute the holy altars by gratifying their evil intentions—we certainly think it highly inconsistent to select for this very purpose, the language of a people from whom we have suffered, and continue to suffer so much persecution.[19]

The potent mix of money and religious honors stirs up volatile language in the petition. The petitioners call men in their own congregation "mischievous and designing men" with "evil intentions." It is not clear exactly to what sort of evil intentions they are referring. Although scholars note that the memorialists were not initially interested in creating a breakaway synagogue, it is rather incendiary language that surely they knew was not going to be welcomed by the Board of Directors.[20]

The Reformers move on to what they perceive as an even bigger problem with the practice of paying for Torah honors. They note that the practice is "idle and absurd indulgence" because according to the by-laws of the congregation, the amount that one pays for Torah honors is subtracted from the yearly subscription [dues]. Therefore the paying for honors raises no money; it is just carried on for the sake of the custom. They do note, however, that some individuals who have previously paid for Torah honors equal to their annual subscription leave the synagogue at the time the honors are sold and go into the courtyard, lest they be pushed into buying them and thus spending over and above their yearly dues. They describe this custom of men leaving to go into the courtyard as "a practice irregular, indecorous, and highly to be censured—because it sets an ill example to our children, and draws upon us the eyes of strangers."[21]

The petitioners do concede that some money is raised through the Torah honors payments since some individuals do buy Torah honors above their yearly subscription, but they call upon the board to devise some other means by which to raise this additional money without continuing to sell honors. Finally, the Reformers suggest that eliminating the practice of selling Torah honors would ultimately be a boon to the synagogue's bottom line because it would induce more people to join the synagogue.

In analyzing the Reformer's attitude towards the custom of paying for honors, the central question is how they came to be so vigorously opposed to the practice when members of their own synagogue, as well as most other synagogues in America, were comfortable mixing money and religion in this way. There is no clear answer as to when and how this change in worldview came about, but we may speculate based on certain statements in the petition.

In the hyperbolic language used to describe the men who carried out the custom—"those mischievous and designing men"—there is a certain note of classic anti-Semitic stereotypes. The Jews in charge of the ritual are depicted as an evil cabal. Money and

Judaism was of course not a neutral topic for nineteenth century Jews. The caricature of Jews as Shylocks obsessed with money was part of American culture at the time.[22] Gary Zola, in his biography of Isaac Harby, the leader of the Charleston Reformers, says Harby was particularly unsettled by Shakespeare's portrayal of Shylock: "Unfortunately, Shakespeare's attack on Shylock branded every Jew as a 'heartless usurer.'"[23]

Perhaps it was out of fear of being labeled as "Shylock Jews" who cared too much about money that the Reformers so vehemently wanted to eliminate this practice of selling Torah honors. Note that one of their central concerns is that the practice of men going into the courtyard to avoid feeling compelled to pay for honors will "draw upon us the eyes of strangers." The Reformers fear that non-Jews may see Jews acting irreverently by leaving a house of worship during prayers—a concern that demonstrates how heavily the influence of their Christian neighbors weighs on the Reformers.

Lou Silberman argues in a significant essay on the Charleston Reformers that the movement for reform was influenced more significantly by the Charleston Protestant community than by the Jewish movement for reform in Germany. Although the Reformers quote from the *Frankfurt Journal* in their petition, the bulk of their arguments seems native-born. Silberman traces the origins of their ideas in part to the Congregational Church in Charleston, which itself experienced a schism over religious reform only a few years earlier and which subsequently split into a Congregationalist and Unitarian church.[24]

Central to his argument is an 1826 essay by the reverend of the Unitarian church[25] on the Constitution of the Reformed Society of Israelites. The essay appeared in the *North American Review*, and it is full of praise for the Reformers. Reverend Gilman writes of the Reform Jews "imbibing the liberal spirit of the age, as to admit the possibility of improvement from within their pale." He also writes of having visited the synagogue and notes approvingly the Reformers' great desire to eliminate the practice of paying for Torah honors. Condemning that practice, he explains: "These Spanish portions of the liturgy are employed only for a particular purpose, namely, to express the amount of *monies offered* for the benefit of the synagogue and its institutions...thus interrupting the prayers and worship with the fiscal concerns of the establishment, and that, too, in a language unknown to almost all present."[26] It is important to bear in mind that Gilman's church did not raise money during services to support the church. Protestant churches of the time utilized pew-rentals for their income and would "pass the plate" only for special missions or specific causes.[27] Gilman's belief that worship should not be interrupted in a foreign language for money concerns seems clear.

It can be concluded that the Charleston Reformers came to see the practice of paying for honors as crass in part as a response to their Christian milieu. Their own fear of connecting worship with money struck too close to the anti-Semitic motifs from which they sought to distance themselves. The use of Spanish only made the practice more threatening and obscure. The Reformers were not immune to caring about synagogue finances, but they make clear in devoting so much of their attention to this issue that disentangling money from worship would be significant in the cause of reform.

To understand the Reformers' attitudes towards this issue in complete context, it is worth briefly examining the schism in Congregation Shearith Israel in New York, which occurred at the exact same time and which also had synagogue honors as an issue.

In 1825 a group of young Jews were clamoring for a change in their synagogue. They viewed with dismay the growing laxity of religious observance and wanted to revitalize Jewish life. Congregation Shearith Israel was the oldest and most established congregation in America. Founded in New York City by the first Jews who came to America, it had always maintained the Sephardic rite. By the 1820s, however, as more Ashkenazic Jews came to New York City, a rift between a younger Ashkenazi group and the older established order became evident.

The young Ashkenazic group published a document—also a petition like the Charleston Reformers'—that laid out its plan for religious renewal. The name of the document is the Constitution and By-laws of the *Hebra Hinuch Nearim* [Society for the Education of Young People]. The seemingly innocuous name does not capture the radical nature of the group. The by-laws make clear that the initial intention of this group was to remain a part of the synagogue, as they say that only members of the synagogue can be a part of the group. But the document reflects the desire to move Shearith Israel toward more religiosity. One article of the constitution says only those people who strictly adhere to observance of the Sabbath and holidays can be members. They also ask for services to be instituted every morning all year long.[28]

Two other articles of the Shearith Israel petition are interesting in light of the Charleston case. In one article, the constitution calls for all synagogue honors to be "distributed in such a manner that every member shall have an equal portion." Another article reduces the minimum offering to be given for the honor of Torah reading from two shillings to six and a quarter cents (It was twelve cents to the shilling, so this is a drop of 75 percent.) It turns out that the practice of paying for Torah honors was at the center of a controversy that led to the founding of the *Hebra Hinuch Nearim*.

As mentioned earlier, Congregation Shearith Israel had instituted a standard amount to be offered for a Torah *aliyah*, the proceeds going to the synagogue's *tzedakah* budget. On the eighth day of Passover in 1825, Barrow Cohen was called for a Torah honor but refused to pay the two shillings, which was a substantial amount of money. Cohen was called to stand trial before the board. He claimed he was ignorant of the custom, as he had seen others not give an offering. The board held that Cohen would not be reprimanded but in the future had to follow synagogue policy. Cohen was irate over the matter, though, and rejected the authority of the board, which subsequently barred Cohen from ever receiving an honor in the synagogue. There seems to have been a bit of political intrigue in this trial, as the minutes of the congregational board spend a good deal of time on the matter. The board ultimately recognized that the two shillings was a substantial amount of money and eliminated the rule. But the damage was seemingly done, as the *Hebra Hinuch Nearim* and ultimately B'nai Jeshurun was formed in the wake of the Cohen controversy.[29]

The schism in Shearith Israel sheds light on the Charleston Reformers by revealing what the latter did *not* argue. The New York group was not concerned about making a monetary offering in synagogue *per se*; rather, the problem for the members of the *Hebra Hinuch Nearim* with paying for Torah honors was that the practice created distinctions within the synagogue. It burdened the less wealthy members of the synagogue and meant that those who could not afford it were not given *aliyot* at all. In an age of increasing democratization within religion, a system that privileged the wealthy to receive sacred honors did not seem in keeping with the times.[30]

In Charleston, the argument against raising money by selling honors was aesthetic, arising in part out of a desire to assimilate into a Christian milieu. The introduction of money sullied the holiness of services. Perhaps it is because this claim is so widely accepted today and seems so self-evident that scholars have glossed over the outrage of the earliest Reformers. While their calls for substantial English in the service is still a source of debate and discussion, most Jewish congregations long ago abandoned the practice of selling honors on the basis of some of the Reformers' logic. While money was neither the only nor the primary cause of their desire to split from Beth Elohim, it was certainly a significant argument in the desire to create a pure Judaism that was modern in both religion and finances.

The widely held view within the Jewish community that selling honors is inappropriate is not without consequences today. It excludes a potential revenue source that had been in use by synagogues for centuries. In contemporary Judaism, it is not unthinkable that the question of whether congregants should pay for particular synagogue privileges and honors could actually come back into focus as synagogues look for ways to raise revenue in times of declining membership. The Christian milieu has now changed dramatically in its understanding of the role of money in worship, as some churches even condone the practice of explicitly praying for wealth.[31] In an American context that validates entrepreneurship and capitalism, the prospect of paying for honors may not seem so outlandish, especially since many synagogues already charge for certain activities and seats to the High Holy Days. Hudnot-Beumler notes in his history of finances and the Protestant church that there is a perception that the way churches have raised money has never changed. But raising revenue, like everything else in church and synagogue life, evolves and changes often in surprising ways.[32]

Notes

1. James Hudnot-Beumler, *In Pursuit of the Almighty's Dollar: A History of Money and American Protestantism* (Chapel Hill: University of North Carolina Press, 2007), xi.
2. There are exceptions to this general rule, notably Leon Jick's *The Americanization of the Synagogue, 1820–1870* (Hanover, NH: Brandeis University Press, 1976) and Hyman Grinstein's *The Rise of the*

Jewish Community in New York, 1654–1860 (Philadelphia: Jewish Publication Society, 1945) both of which significantly utilize economic perspectives.

3. James Hagy, *This Happy Land: The Jews of Colonial and Antebellum Charleston* (Tuscaloosa: University of Alabama Press, 1993), 16.
4. "Memorial," reprinted in L.C. Moise, *Biography of Isaac Harby* (Columbia, SC: R. L. Bryan, 1931).
5. Works on the origins of the Charleston community include: Barnett Elzas, *The Reformed Society of Israelites* (New York: Bloch Publishing Company, 1916); Robert Liberles, "Conflict Over Reform: The Case of Congregation Beth Elohim, Charleston, South Carolina," in *American Synagogue: A Sanctuary Transformed*, ed. Jack Wertheimer (New York: Basic, 1993), 274–96; Lou Silberman, *American Impact: Judaism in the United States in the Early Nineteenth Century* (Syracuse: Syracuse University Press, 1964); Michael Meyer, *Response to Modernity* (Detroit: Wayne State University Press, 1995), 228–34. Elzas does make a kind of economic argument in his contention that the Reformers were the most influential and aristocratic group in the synagogue, but this argument has been refuted by Liberles and does not appear in the contemporary literature.
6. Jonathan Sarna, *American Judaism* (New Haven: Yale University Press, 2004), 54–61.
7. Meyer, *Response to Modernity*, 230.
8. Hyman Grinstein, *The Rise of the Jewish Community in New York, 1654–1860* (Philadelphia: Jewish Publication Society of America, 1947), 480–81.
9. Ibid., 532 n. 9.
10. I.e., Simchat Torah.
11. Joseph Colon, *Shealot U'tsheuvot*, no. 9.
12. Ismar Elbogen, *Jewish Liturgy: A Comprehensive History*, trans. Raymond Scheindlin (Philadelphia: Jewish Publication Society of America, 1993) 142, 424 n. 117
13. Ibid., 424 n. 117.
14. Quoted in Lance Sussman, *Isaac Leeser and the Making of American Judaism* (Detroit: Wayne State University Press, 1995), 135.
15. The incident is reported in many places, see Sefton Temkin, *Creating American Reform Judaism: The Life and Times of Isaac Mayer Wise* (Portland: Vallentine, Mitchell and Co., 1998), 72–75, which analyzes the event with particular reference to the buying of the honor.
16. Liberles, "Conflict Over Reform," 280.
17. Sarna, *American Judaism*, 58.
18. "Memorial," 52.

19. "Memorial," 55.
20. Liberles, "Conflict Over Reform," 286.
21. "Memorial," 56.
22. Leonard Dinnerstein, a historian of anti-Semitism, quotes the governor of Mississippi in 1837 speaking in reference to Baron Rothschild as saying, "The blood of Judas and Shylock flows through his veins, and he unites the qualities of both his countrymen." Leonard Dinnerstein, "A Note on Southern Attitudes Towards Jews," *Jewish Social Studies* 32, no. 1 (1970): 44.
23. Gary Zola, *Isaac Harby of Charleston 1788–1828: Jewish Reformer and Intellectual* (Tuscaloosa: University of Alabama Press, 1994), 117.
24. Lou Silberman, *American Impact*.
25. The church would only officially become Unitarian some years later, but it was Unitarian in spirit at this time.
26. "Review of *The Constitution of the Reformed Society of Israelites, for Promoting True Principles of Judaism According to Its Purity and Spirit,*" *North American Review* 23, no. 52 (July 1826): 67–79. The author of the review is anonymous, but Silberman notes in the above cited article that the review is certainly by Rev. Gilman's hand.
27. George Edwards, *A History of the Independent or Congregational Church of Charleston South Carolina* (Boston: Pilgrim Press, 1947), 66.
28. *The Constitution and Bye-laws of the* Hebra Hinuch Nearim, American Jewish Historical Society.
29. Grinstein, *The Rise of the Jewish Community*, 41–49; Shearith Israel Board of Trustees Notes, 149–180, American Jewish Archives.
30. On the increasing democratization of religious institutions in the early nineteenth century, the standard work is Nathan Hatch, *The Democratization of American Christianity* (New Haven: Yale University Press, 1989); see Sarna, *American Judaism*, 54–61, for democratization's influence on synagogues.
31. There is a large popular literature on this subject. As an example of this movement within the Christian church, see Bruce Wilkinson, *The Prayer of Jabez* (Oregon: Multnomah Publishers Inc., 2000), which sold millions of copies on the premise that praying for wealth is acceptable.
32. Hudnot-Beumler, *In Pursuit of the Almighty's Dollar*, xi.

The Decline and Fall of the Interest Ban[1]

Hillel Gamoran

The Torah prohibits Israelites from lending to each other on interest.[2] The purpose of the law against interest was to prevent increasing the debts of poor Israelites; the biblical law did not take business loans into consideration.

The Period of the Talmud

But in the period of the Tannaim, in the first two centuries of the Common Era, manufacturing and commerce increased,[3] and there developed the need for loans of a business nature. Shopkeepers and animal breeders needed capital for their enterprises, and tradesmen of all sorts required credit to carry on their dealings. There also were wealthy persons, usually large landowners or established merchants, with idle money. They wished to put their funds to work. The question thus arose as to whether the biblical law against interest, designed for the protection of the poor, would stand in the way of profitable business loans during the period of the Tannaim.

The Tannaim did find a way for one to give money to his fellow and to gain a profit. It was through an investment.[4] Unlike a loan, where the borrower assumed all of the risk, with an investment, the investor assumed 50 percent of any loss. He also shared profits equally with the working partner. Because the investor risked a portion of his capital, which was not the case with a loan, the Rabbis permitted him to profit if the venture proved successful. It was the risk that distinguished the investment from a loan and that made it legal in tannaitic law.

HILLEL GAMORAN (NY56) is the rabbi emeritus of Beth Tikvah Congregation in Hoffman Estates, Illinois where he served for thirty-four years. For the past fourteen years, he has taught rabbinic literature at the University of Washington in Seattle.

In the amoraic period, in the third, fourth, and fifth centuries, the center of Jewish life shifted to Babylonia. In Babylonia, the half-profit investment became widely used. It gave investors an opportunity for profit, which was forbidden with loans, and it provided businessmen with the capital they needed to carry out their enterprises. The half-profit investment was called an *iska*, and it was considered to be one-half a loan and one-half a deposit.[5] The Babylonian sages looked upon the *iska* as a fine Rabbinical enactment. It grew in popularity, satisfying the Rabbis that the interest laws were not being violated, yet meeting the demands of the economy for credit.

In the period of the Geonim, about 650 to 1050, the question arose as to whether it was possible for one to invest in an *iska* and be free of all liability in case the investment failed. The Geonim consistently responded in the negative. The investor, they ruled, was responsible for the deposit (i.e., half of the investment), and if the business venture went bad, he could lose half of his investment.[6]

The Period of the Rishonim

In the eleventh century, Rabbi Isaac Alfasi expressed a clear-cut defense of the geonic position. Alfasi declared that the recipient of the investment should guard it carefully, but he pointed out that "one who received an *iska* was not able, wherever he went, to guard it in the ground. Therefore, if he acted more or less in the way that merchants did, then he was not...liable" for the deposit portion of an *iska*.[7]

In the twelfth century, Rabbi Abraham ben David of Posquieres,[8] known as Rabad, apparently using Alfasi's ruling as a springboard to provide investors with a technique for avoiding all liability for an *iska*, wrote in a responsum:[9]

> If someone wants to give his fellow an *iska*, in a legal manner, for a set amount of time, let him do it this way. The investor should say to the recipient,...."Lend it only with good pledges of silver and gold and always put the money under the ground in order to guard it from fire and thieves."...And after the investor makes these stipulations with the recipient, then the recipient may lend in any way that he wishes,...for he knows that the investor stipulated with him in order to place all of the liability on him should he deviate [from the stipulations].

In short, Rabad was suggesting a contract that both parties knew to be a legal fiction. The manager received the capital that enabled him to trade, and the investor had the opportunity to profit while being relieved of liability for his investment. The contract achieved this by stipulating conditions for the care of the lender's stake that all parties involved knew could not and would not be fulfilled.

People who wanted to make money with money found a drawback in the *iska*. The investor risked losing half of his investment. Rabad provided the solution: an *iska* that made the working partner liable for both the deposit portion of the *iska* and, of course, for the loan portion. Thus, although, for centuries, Rabbinic authorities had crafted the *iska* in such a way as to prevent it from resulting in usury, in the twelfth century, the restrictions were relaxed and the *iska* was allowed to become a profitable, risk-free investment.

Although Rabad's position, clearing investors of liability for their investments, took hold among most Rabbinic jurists in the thirteenth and fourteenth centuries,[10] it was opposed by some[11] and was still a matter of debate in the fifteenth century.

The clearest expression of granting permission for a partnership agreement that allowed the investor to profit without risking his principal came from the pen of Rabbi Israel Isserlein in the fifteenth century.[12] Isserlein was told, in an inquiry,[13] that Reuben wanted to profit by giving money to Simon "while being almost completely certain that he would not lose any of his principal." "How," asked the questioner, "might this be accomplished legally?"

Isserlein began his response by expressing his reservations about answering the question. He explained that, while the questioner's purpose could, indeed, be achieved, "I am afraid... that by seeking strategies to allow business dealings with interest, the words of the Torah will become a laughingstock."

However, in spite of his concern, Isserlein believed that his views were correct, and he proceeded to answer the question. He said that "a person could give money to his fellow on a half-profit basis and could contract with him not to lend it except on pledges of silver or gold and to bury them in the ground, and then the liability would be the investor's. But if he lends in other ways, then the recipient will be liable." And Isserlein added that "even though everyone knows that it is not at all the intention of the investor or of the recipient that the stipulation [to bury the pledges in the ground] be fulfilled...nevertheless it is allowed." The unique feature of

Isserlein's response was his open admission that the contract was a subterfuge and that the parties were well aware that the working partner would not live up to the stipulations. The stipulations were inserted with a wink and a nod by all concerned, knowing that they were simply a way of allowing the investor to place all of the risk on the recipient.

Isserlein provided yet another method whereby the investor could place the entire liability onto the shoulders of the manager. This is how it worked: The contract would state that Simon, the working partner, accepts liability for gross negligence,

> and he also accepts upon himself that he is not to be believed even with an oath on the Torah, and even with witnesses, and even if there are a hundred who testify that he was not greatly negligent. Only if the rabbi and the cantor and similar people who are residents of the city and are familiar with the business dealings in the city will testify [that he was not negligent] will he be believed...
>
> And in this way will his principal be secure as he always wishes. For if it is lost, Reuben [the investor] may claim that it was lost intentionally, and Simon will be able to uphold his claim only with the testimony of the rabbi and the cantor. And it is almost entirely certain that they will not know all [of the details regarding] the liability.
>
> And it is permitted to stipulate as has been said...even though surely neither of them believes that the conditions will be fulfilled, and they make these stipulations only in order to take interest in a legal way.

Perhaps we should not be surprised that the Rabbis devised a legal way to allow profitable investments in partnerships. Muslim jurists, in their day, found a way for the Islamic faithful to pursue their business activities without hindrance from their laws against usury, and Christian theologians provided ways for bankers to lend on interest with the Church's blessing. Why, then, should not the Rabbis similarly have devised a means to allow the economic activity of their day to proceed within the framework of the halachah?

As the period of the Rishonim drew to a close, investors had within their grasp a halachically sanctioned means by which to profit from their investments without risking the loss of their principal. Just as in the case of a loan where the borrower was completely responsible for any loss, so in the case of an *iska*, if the proper stipulations were included in the contract, the recipient could be held completely responsible for the investment. But whereas any profit from a loan was forbidden as usury, profit from an *iska* was deemed to be a legitimate business gain.

A Set Profit Goal

In the period after Isserlein, an important change was made in the *iska* contract. This change had its origin in the Jerusalem Talmud,[14] where Rabbi Eliezer gave money to someone on condition that he (Eliezer) would profit from the investment until Chanukah; after Chanukah, all of the profit would go to the worker.

The innovation in the *Y'rushalmi*, that the investment be divided into two time periods, was used as the basis for a ruling by Rabbi Joseph Karo[15] in the *Shulchan Aruch*. But instead of setting a *fixed time* when the investment would be transformed from a deposit to a loan, this ruling in the *Shulchan Aruch*[16] set a *fixed amount of profit* the worker needed to reach; only then would the funds become a loan with all of the profit (and liability) becoming the worker's.

The idea of establishing a fixed sum for the profit due the investor was included in a sixteenth century responsum of Rabbi Moses Isserles[17] (Rama).[18] Rama allowed the lender of 800 gold pieces to specify in his contract with borrowers that at the end of the year, instead of dividing the profit, the borrowers could pay him 1,000 pieces, or 25 more per 100 coins. This amount was not interest; rather, it was profit on an investment, specified contractually at 25 percent—and it was permitted by Rama.

In any case, near the end of the sixteenth century, Rabbi Isaiah Menahem ben Isaac, better known as Rabbi Mendel Avigdors (Maharam),[19] assumed the task of writing a partnership contract to serve as a form for anyone who wished to engage in an investment transaction. What is remarkable about the contract designed by Maharam is that it included the amount of the expected profit due the investor. If the investor's share of the profit at the end of the year was greater than that sum, then the recipient was allowed to keep the excess. However, if the profit was less than the designated sum, then the recipient would be required to take a rare, stern oath to affirm that fact.

For all intents and purposes, the investor's profit was guaranteed. As one sage put it, "Even if the recipient knows afterwards that he did not profit, or even if he lost, he is allowed to repay the investor the principal and the profit to which they agreed."[20] Setting a specific sum to be paid to the investor became a standard part of the investment contract. The publication of this contract gave the business community what it sorely desired, a halachically permissible way to invest funds with the assurance of profit, sanctioned by one of the foremost Rabbinic authorities of the time.

Rabbinic law had come a long way. The authorities of the Mishnah had all agreed that fixed interest was a firm biblical prohibition to be roundly condemned. By the sixteenth century, however, it was customary for contracts to include a specified sum to be paid to the investor. True, it was an investment, not a loan, and the specified sum was profit, not interest; but the practical effect was that the investor's profit was assured by a legal contract.

The contract of Rabbi Mendel spread in usage throughout the Jewish communities of Eastern Europe and became known as the *Heter Iska* (permission for an investment partnership) Contract of Maharam. Using Maharam's *iska* contract meant that the investor would definitely recover his principal, and, in all likelihood, he would also receive the sum specified in the contract as his profit. Although, according to halachic categories, this was not technically a loan with guaranteed interest, it functioned as such in practice.

The Generic *Heter Iska*

The use of the *heter iska* for loans of all sorts became normative practice within the Jewish community. But there was a problem. In the case of a Jewish-owned bank, writing a *heter iska* every time the bank issued a loan was a cumbersome task. To ease this problem, Rabbi Shalom Mordecai Shvadron (1835–1911, Maharsham)[21] approved the writing of a generic *heter iska*,[22] a contract signed in court by the owners of a Jewish bank indicating that all of the loans given by that bank would be made in accordance with the rules of *heter iska*. After this declaration was signed in court, Maharsham publicized the matter by announcing it in the synagogues and in the houses of study. With this action, Maharsham declared that when one borrowed from that bank, it was as if he had explicitly stipulated that the loan was executed according to a *heter iska* and that the text of the contract was in the court.

Maharsham was a renowned and respected religious authority. His introduction of the generic *heter iska* opened up a new avenue for loans among Jews. With a formal declaration by the bank's authorities and with the approval of the court, it was no longer necessary for each and every borrower to complete an individual contract. The *heter iska* was filed with the court and then one could borrow on interest from the bank. There was no necessity to complete a separate contract. The one that the court held applied to all loans issued by the bank.

The generic *heter iska* of Maharsham, designed early in the twentieth century for use by Jewish-owned banks, was followed in 1924 by a *heter iska* prepared by Rabbi Ezriel Meir Eiger (1878–1943) for all Jewish businesses.[23] Eiger contended that not only banks, but all Jewish businessmen needed a generic *heter iska*.[24] Two problems arose, however: For one thing, many people, even many conscientious Torah-abiding Jews, were not always in a position to write a *heter iska* for every loan. Secondly, people who would normally enter into a *heter iska* at times simply forgot to do so. Therefore, Eiger proposed that whenever a Jew entered the world of business, he should write a generic *heter iska* that would last him a lifetime. This would keep him from transgression in case he was forgetful or, for some reason, was unable to write one when engaging in a loan transaction.

In 1974, Rabbi Moses Feinstein (1895–1986)[25] wrote a responsum outlining the terms to be included in a generic *heter iska* for banks.[26] He allowed banks both to lend and to accept deposits, to charge a fee to borrowers, and to grant an increase to depositors. All this could be accomplished through the issuance of a generic *heter iska* by the directors of the bank. Feinstein explained that the *heter iska* would work even if the borrower did not know about the *heter iska*.

Rabbi Feinstein wrote his responsum to apply to a bank in Rockland County, New York, but the greatest use of the generic *heter iska* today is in Israeli banks. It is simply not practical for Jewish-owned banks that cater to Jewish customers to deal with a *heter iska* contract every time someone makes a deposit or takes a loan. For this reason, the generic *heter iska* is widely used in Israel's banks. Each bank has its own *heter iska* text with formal rabbinic approval. While its customers, if they are unaware that their business is being conducted under a *heter iska*, may regard their borrowing or lending as simply a loan with interest, the transaction is nevertheless halachically compliant and is executed with the approval of the highest rabbinical authorities in Israel.

Conclusion

While the Bible shows its concern for poor borrowers by banning borrowing and lending at interest, in the post-biblical period, the law against interest almost immediately engendered pushback from the business community. One might imagine that the biblical law designed to help the needy would be limited in its application to the poor and not be imposed upon the broader world of business and commerce. In the two thousand years since the close of the Bible, however, no rabbi or sage has ever suggested that the biblical law pertains only to loans to the poor, while those engaged in business are exempt from the ban on interest. Indeed, no halachic authority was prepared to assert that, in certain circumstances, borrowing or lending on interest should be allowed.

So the Rabbis addressed the tension between biblical law and practical necessity through the art of interpretation. While they did not rule that the law should be ignored, they subverted the law by interpreting it in such a way as to meet the desired goals of community members. By interpreting the biblical ban on interest in such a way as to permit it, they were following a long-established tradition of legal flexibility.

Examples of such flexibility abound throughout Jewish history. For instance, Hillel had permitted debts to be collected on the seventh year, contrary to an explicit biblical prohibition, by allowing the court to collect them from borrowers on behalf of lenders.[27] Dealing in gentile wine was forbidden in the Talmud, but Rashi allowed it on grounds that the Talmudic law applied to non-Jews who used wine to offer libations to idols. Since non-Jews did not use wine for such purposes in Rashi's day, he relaxed the prohibition.[28] Rabbeinu Tam circumvented the injunction against having servants heat Jewish homes on the Sabbath by explaining that the servants themselves benefited from such labor and that the comfort afforded to their Jewish masters was only incidental.[29] Solomon Luria, when faced with the fact that women were widely engaged in business and commerce, interpreted the Talmudic prohibition against looking at or speaking with women to apply only to men who could not control their desires.[30]

In the case of interest, it was a matter of calling a loan an investment. While lending on interest was forbidden, investing for profit was permitted. It was forbidden to lend $100 and stipulate that the borrower return $110, but one was allowed to invest $100 in a partnership agreement and stipulate that a profit of $10 be returned along with the principal. The *heter iska* was the culmination of centuries of struggle with the tension between the prohibition against interest, on the one hand, and a credit society, in which borrowing and lending were everyday occurrences, on the other.

Through the medium of the *heter iska*, a Jew can lend money to his co-religionist and establish a fixed rate for periodic interest payments while remaining compliant with the letter of the law. A Jew can walk into a Jewish-owned bank, deposit his money, receive his regular interest payments unaware that his deposit is governed by a *heter iska*, and still be acting within the framework of Jewish law approved by leading halachic authorities.

The Rabbis faced the challenge of preserving the laws of the Torah while upholding the needs of the Jewish community. The law against lending on interest provides an excellent example of how they used their interpretive skills to uphold the law while allowing business and commercial life to flourish.

Notes

1. This article is based on the author's book *Jewish Law in Transition: How Economic Forces Overcame the Prohibition against Lending on Interest* (Cincinnati: Hebrew Union College Press, 2008).
2. Exod. 22:24; Deut. 23:20–21; Lev. 25:35–37.
3. See Gedalyahu Alon, *The Jews in Their Land in the Talmudic Age* (Cambridge, Massachusetts: Harvard University Press, 1994), 6–8, 152–75; Hayim Lapin, *Economy, Geography and Provincial History in Later Roman Palestine* (Tubingen: Mohr Siebeck, 2001), 172–75.
4. *Mishnah Bava M'tzia* 5:4–5; *Tosefta Bava M'tzia* 4:11–22.
5. BT *Bava M'tzia* 104b–105a.
6. *Sha'are Tsedek*, part 4, gate 8, #5; Ezriel Hildesheimer, ed., *Sefer Halakhot Gedolot* (Jerusalem: Mekitse Nirdamim, 1971), 406.
7. Isaac Alfasi, *She'elot U-teshuvot Ha-rav Yitshak Alsfasi*, Dov Zvi Rothstein, ed. (New York: Makhon Zvi Le-moreshet Gedole Yisrael, 1975), #75.
8. In Provence.

9. Abraham ben David of Posquieres, *Teshuvot U-fesakim*, Joseph Kafih, ed. (Jerusalem: Mosad Harav Kook, 1964), #140; *Temim De'im* (Warsaw, 1897), #60.
10. Isaac of Vienna, *Or Zarua*, (Zhitomir, 1862), part 3, *Bava M'tzia* #342; Jacob Hazzan, *Etz Hayyim*, vol. 3, Israel Brody, ed. (Jerusalem: Mossad Harav Kook, 1967), 152; Meir of Rothenburg, *She'elot U-teshuvot Maharam ben Barukh* (Budapest: Defus Prague, 1895), #806; Menahem ben Solomon (Ha-meiri), *Bet Ha-Behirah al Masekhet Bava Metsia* (Jerusalem: Mekitse Nirdamim, 1959), 104b, 388.
11. Solomon Duran, *Yakhin U-voaz, She'elot U-teshuvot*, part 2 (Levorno 1782), #23; Joseph Colon, *She'elot U-teshuvot Maharik Ha-yeshanot* (Jerusalem: Oraysoh, 1988), Shoresh #119.
12. In Austria.
13. Israel Isserlein, *Terumat Ha-deshen*, Samuel Avitan, ed. (Jerusalem, 1991), #302.
14. JT *Bava M'tzia* 5:6.
15. 1488–1575 in Palestine.
16. Joseph Karo, *Shulhan Arukh, Yoreh De'ah*, #167:1.
17. In Poland.
18. Moses Isserles, *She'elot U-teshuvot Ha-rama* (Jerusalem: Feldheim, 1971), #80.
19. In Poland. Mendel was a common name for the Hebrew, Menahem. Avigdors was his father-in-law's name, which was customary for a young man in his time to adopt.
20. Solomon Ganzfried, *Kitsur Shulhan Arukh* (Jerusalem: Mosad Harav Kook, 1974), #66:3.
21. In Poland.
22. Shalom Mordecai Shvadron, *She'elot U-teshuvot Maharsham* (Jerusalem: Mekhon Hatam Sofer, 1973–1989), 1:20, s.v. "Uv'guf."
23. In Poland.
24. Ezriel Meir Eiger, *Takanat Rabim* (Warsaw, 1930; Bene Berak, 1956), Introduction.
25. In New York.
26. Moses Feinstein, *Igrot Moshe, Yoreh De'ah* (Brooklyn: Moria, 1982) 3:41.
27. BT *Gittin* 36a.
28. Solomon ben Isaac, *She'elot U-teshuvot Rashi* (Bene Berak, 1980), #58, #327.
29. Jacob ben Meir Tam, *Sefer Ha-yashar Le-rabeinu Tam* (Jerusalem: Simon Schlesinger, 1959), #286.
30. Solomon Luria, *Yam Shel Shelomo* (Jerusalem, 1996), *Kiddushin* 4:4, 4:25.

Poetry

In the Black Night
Vayishlach

John L. Rosove

In the black night
the river runs cold
slowly passing me by
over formerly sharp edged stones
worn smooth by centuries of churning,
as if through earthy veins—
and I Jacob, alone,
shiver and wait
to meet my brother
and daylight.

Will there be war?
And will the angels carry my soul
up the rungs of the ladder
leaving my blood
to soak the earthly crust?

A presence!?
And I struggle yet again
as if in my mother's womb
and in my dreams.

We played together as children once,
my brother Esau and me,
as innocents,
and I confess tonight
how I wronged him
and wrenched from him his birthright
as this Being has done to me
between my thighs.

JOHN L. ROSOVE (NY79) is senior rabbi of Temple Israel of Hollywood, Los Angeles.

I was so young,
driven by ego and need,
blinded by ambition,
my mother's dreams
and my father's silence.

I so craved to be first born,
adored by my father,
to assume his place when he died
that my name be remembered
and define a people.

How Esau suffered and wailed,
and I didn't care.
Whatever his dreams
they were nothing to me—
my heart was hard—
his life be damned!

But, after all these years
I've learned that Esau and I
each alone is
a *palga gufa*—a half soul
without the other—
torn away
as two souls separated at creation
seeking reunification
in a sea of souls—
the yin missing the yang—
the dark and light never to touch—
the mind divorced from body—
the soul in exile—
without a beating bleating heart
to witness—
and no access to the thirty-two paths
to carry us together
up the ladder
and through the spheres.

It's come to this!
To struggle again—
To live or die.

Tonight
I'm ready for death
or submission.

Compassionate One:
protect Esau and your servant—
my brother and me
as one—
and return us to each other.

El na r'fa na lanu!
Grant us peace and rest!
I'm very tired.

Book Reviews

The Legacy of Our Reform Kibbutzim: Can We Renew the Dream?
A Review Essay

Debra Goldstein

Reviewing

Light in the Arava? Yahel: Dialogue and a Joint Undertaking between the Kibbutz Movement and the Reform Movement by Gidon Elad (English edition, Israel: Tzell Hatamar and Kibbutz Yahel, 2008), 320 pp.

Zion in the Desert: American Jews in Israel's Reform Kibbutzim by William F. S. Miles (Albany: State University of New York Press, 2007), 240 pp.

As an active participant of ARZA for quite some time, I am familiar with its recently renewed study of, and struggle with, the questions of What is "Reform Zionism"? and What is the place of *aliyah* in today's American Reform world? The last several years have seen reinvigorated efforts to introduce to American Reform Jews an idea of Zionism as our mission to help shape the democratic and pluralistic nature of Israeli society and to float a new concept of *aliyah* to see it more as opportunities for recurring, extended, and deeper life experiences in Israel. So it was with piqued interest that I dove into these two recently published books. They both tell the story of an earlier unique period of intense Reform Zionist connection to Israel, but each from totally different perspectives that create a perfect complement to one another. And, at this time when the Progressive movement in Israel is poised for important recognition and growth opportunities, can we learn from the past histories recounted in these books to take greater advantage of this present potential?

Gidon Elad's book was originally written in Hebrew in 1997. It was first translated into English in 2000 (shortly before Elad's death), with later further and final editing by Michael Livni in 2008. Elad, a sabra, a founder of Kibbutz Hatzerim in the northwestern Negev, and a leader in the kibbutz movement, was first and foremost a leader in informal education both in Israel and the Diaspora. He was a leader of the Israeli Scout movement, a *sh'liach* to the British Habonim in the 1950s, to Young Judea in the United States in the 1960s, and to the Reform Movement in the 1970s (the second one after Michael Livni). He understood both worlds and became a bridge between them, and he was thus personally involved with the process he recounts. His insightful monograph traces the evolution of the gradual engagement process between those two originally diametrically opposed historical movements as they began to supplement the lack of each other.

In his research, Elad attempts to answer a mystery: Given the very different responses to modernity that Zionism and Reform represented, and given the minimal, sporadic contact between them throughout most of the twentieth century, what factors occurred or coalesced in the early 1970s to create the phenomenon of a Reform kibbutz, and what can we learn from the story?

Elad starts with a background on the early individual contacts between individual Reform rabbis and representatives of the kibbutz/Labor movements: Judah Magnes and Manya Shochat in 1906–1907; the 1926–1927 CCAR Committee to study the feasibility of establishing a Reform congregation in Palestine; the Labor Zionist efforts of individuals like Rabbi Samuel Wohl and Rabbi Edward Israel; and the 1937 speech by Rabbi Maurice Eisendrath regarding how the kibbutz workers were living the values of Reform Judaism and that Reform could meet their inner spiritual needs beyond socialism. While these activities began building the foundations for cooperation between the kibbutz movement and Reform, no such cooperation developed at that time. For Elad, the fact that the Reform leadership and rank-and-file rabbis remained more interested in continuing its integration into American society, and the common Israeli belief at the time (including in the kibbutz movement) that Reform are "evil angels of assimilation" or is an abnormal mutation of Judaism, both worked against the possibility and growth of cooperation. He believed the contacts did, however, help in the adoption of the 1937 Columbus Platform and the "Zionisation" of Reform by the time of the establishment of the

State of Israel. Greater cooperation would not happen until after the Six-Day War.

Elad sees the Six-Day War was a watershed of sorts in that it inspired an empowerment of Jewish identity and caused more engagement with Israel in the American Jewish community as a whole. In the Reform Movement, it inspired Rabbi Richard Hirsch, then Director of the RAC, to write a memorandum in September 1967 noting that the realization of, and connection to, a Jewish life in Israel has "implanted new idealism, purpose, and hope in America Jewry." He proposed a plan of formal and informal educational activities of various lengths in Israel for children, teens, adults, and rabbis and other Jewish professionals, advocating a new conceptual approach based on using personal connection to Israel as a resource for enhancing Jewish identity and sense of peoplehood among the American Reform Jewish public. This memo led to the creation of the first budgeted Israel Committee within the UAHC at its November Biennial that year, to pursue activities in line with Rabbi Hirsch's proposals, "including, if possible, settlements under the auspices of progressive Judaism." That wording was purposely vague and the strongest Hirsch could get passed, but for him, for Reform to gain a real presence in Israel, it was important to show secular Israelis that we had a universal Jewish message, and to do so, Reform had to be built through and by Israeli society—like the core Israeli society, through the soil, through kibbutz. Even with this wording, the decision was a major shift from the conventional congregational approach of the Reform Movement, but it would still take several years to bear any fruit.

The bulk of Elad's book gives us a detailed, behind-the-scenes look at the ensuing meetings and machinations of a core of dedicated leaders to create a "living" Reform presence in Israel, focusing on the catalyzing roles of Rabbis Hank Skirball and Allen Levine in Israel, and Rabbi Stephen Schafer at the UAHC Youth Division working with them and their Labor Zionist colleagues. We also get a look at the practical political and ideological thinking behind the kibbutz movement's efforts to reach out to the American Reform Movement, including a feeling of ideological and spiritual vacuum among some second- and third-generation kibbutz members. It was this latter searching (which would become more pronounced after the 1973 Yom Kippur War) that created a point of meeting for the two groups. In March 1970, at the first CCAR conference in Israel, the invited kibbutz leader Moshe Kerem stressed to the plenum that Reform would not be able to establish anything in the Land of Israel unless it actually connected to the land, and not just established American-type synagogues for American immigrants in Jerusalem and Tel Aviv. This message reiterated the earlier one of Rabbi Hirsch and was coupled with an offer to actually work together. This led to the historic first "official" meeting between the Reform Movement and the United Kibbutz Movement in August 1971.

Elad makes us privy to the personalities and relationships of the parties at this meeting from the conference notes and his extensive interviews. This first meeting was conducted all in Hebrew and stressed the group's commonalities of "esteem for social justice and the desire to introduce innovations into our spiritual life." They discussed issues of Jewish identity, tradition, the realization of Jewish values within their communities, and how both groups attempt to express the synthesis of particularism and universalism. Beyond discussion, the meeting began to develop a joint program for cooperation based on a shared ideological basis, including advocacy to establish a Reform kibbutz. This meeting was a major rapprochement by both movements and a huge step forward in Reform rediscovery of peoplehood and a deeper, more meaningful relationship to Israel beyond political and financial support. (This was also the time when the HUC-JIR Year in Israel program had just started.) But from Elad's perspective, he saw a big difference in how the Reform Movement perceived this development: The core leadership saw it as the beginning of a new Jewish direction and coalition to create a legitimate place for Reform in Israel, while the rank-and-file rabbis seemed to see it more as just an additional, albeit important, educational resource, especially for youth. This difference would affect the future development of the kibbutzim: the core leadership often had to act unofficially and under the radar because it lacked deep support, and the necessary Zionist educational foundations throughout the Movement that could attract young adults to make *aliyah* were not created.

In addition to detailed chronicling of the activities and political jockeying of the next several years until the establishment of Kibbutz Yahel in November 1976, Elad offers a look at the unique issues that the young American and Israeli *chalutzim* faced and his analysis of the shortcomings of the endeavor. Unlike their American counterparts, the American Reform kibbutzniks had to struggle with how to create a liberal religious community of *total life*, not just a community of ritual/worship. What would be the role of halachah in making daily, practical decisions of Reform communal life? How were they to accommodate the personal autonomy characteristic of American Reform to a kibbutz communal responsibility lifestyle? There was a continuing tension between fostering "communal cultural life" and "life according to the way of life of Progressive Judaism," especially for the secular Israeli members, and particularly because the young founding members did not necessarily share the religious/ideological vision of the rabbinic organizers. (The philosophical discussion of these issues in Elad's book is expanded on a more personal level in Miles's book.) They had no examples to follow, and Elad questions whether they had enough guidance from the UAHC or the IMPJ as to their visions and goals or enough preliminary Zionist ideological and educational grounding to ease their way.

Although the chronology is sometimes choppy and one might occasionally get bogged down in myriad names and affiliations, Elad offers a compelling insider's perspective to those formative years. And it often takes an "outsider" to American Reform to shed light on our challenges. The question mark in the title is telling. An ongoing partnership with the kibbutz movement never materialized: the close cooperation starting in the late 1970s between Rabbi Alex Schindler and Musa Charif (a leader of the Labor Zionist kibbutz movement and a rising star in the Labor Party) did not penetrate deeper into either movement and Charif died tragically in a car accident in 1982; the fervor of Rabbis Skirball, Levine, and Schafer was not reflected in the rest of the Youth Division nor deep within the UAHC, and they retired in the closing decades of the century; and the economic crises in Israel starting the mid-1980s caused an implosion of the kibbutz movement. Despite the questionable future when Elad finished his research in the 1980s, he was not pessimistic: "In the final analysis, it is not the political or the congregational struggle that will determine the legitimacy of the Reform approach in the minds of Israelis, but rather its ability to become part and parcel of the internal Israeli social agenda. In that sense Yahel was a breakthrough." But only time will tell.

Distinct from, and as a complement to, Elad's historical/political account, William Miles's *Zion in the Desert* offers us a personal/

sociological view of the development of Reform Kibbutzim Yahel and Lotan. Indeed, in his preface, he admits to working out some of his own unresolved Zionist feelings while writing the book and calls this an "ethno-autobiography: exploring one's self through the study of one's ethnic peers." His portraits of the places and people of Yahel and Lotan, from their inception until today, supplement and give "flesh" to the political history of Elad and the personal stories that were just touched on there. Through in-depth interviews and photos, we get a sense of the smell, look, and feel of the kibbutzim—their struggles, triumphs, and challenges—through the eyes of the author and the residents. It is well structured and easy to read (and for some of us Boomers with our own unresolved Zionist feelings, easy to identify with). Through the flow of chapters, we explore why the American members came, the various economic and personal crises faced, why they stayed, how they measured the success of their religious/communal mix, the differences/rivalries between Yahel and Lotan, and why some left. In many respects it is a love story. For Miles,

> The Reform Kibbutz is a time capsule of idealism, tempered by middle age...[T]hese middle-class American baby boomers traded in their diasporic identities for Israeli selves. They have done what I cannot: recreate themselves as Hebrew-speaking, desert-dwelling, unambiguous Zionists. In their American-style liberalism and idealism, I can still feel traces of my own generation and peer group. But it is in the sabrams, the [American Israeli next generation] bicultural kibbutz kids, that I see a completely new native face of Israel. It is a good face, a hopeful face, a generous face.

Both of these books, alone and together, give us a picture of a particular moment in history when factors coalesced and committed leaders took advantage of the opportunity to create a living Reform presence in Israel. That particular moment is gone, but Kibbutz Yahel and Kibbutz Lotan are still here, having weathered economic crises in their own ways, with visions for the future. There is also still that yearning in both the Israeli and American public for a deeper spiritual, Jewish meaning to their lives that was the original catalyst for meeting. We also have many, many more congregations, schools, and social institutions in Israel now. And the Progressive movement in Israel is currently poised for significant government recognition opportunities. Will we learn the lessons of our first experiment so vividly described in these books? Will we as a Movement have the deeper commitment and take advantage anew of the present moment of opportunity to build the necessary Reform Zionist ideological and educational infrastructures here and in Israel that would teach Israeli youth and adults about Reform and that could motivate our people to volunteer for programs in Israel and envisage long-term connection and possible settlement—to build the Reform presence in Israel that would become integral to our own Judaism, thus fulfilling our societies' mutual yearnings?

RABBI DEBRA GOLDSTEIN (NY07) came to the rabbinate after a career as an attorney. She is currently working for the Carl and Dorothy Bennett Center for Judaic Studies at Fairfield University, Fairfield, CT.

Jewish Law in Transition
by Hillel Gamoran
(Cincinnati: Hebrew Union College Press, 2008), 196 pp.

Simply, but inadequately, stated, *Jewish Law in Transition* by Hillel Gamoran deals with a very specific, particular topic: the transformation over many hundreds of years, in Jewish religious practice, of a biblical law that strictly prohibited the taking of interest on loans into its direct opposite; namely, business arrangements equivalent to the taking of interest! Or, as the subtitle puts it: *How Economic Forces Overcame the Prohibition against Lending on Interest.*

In the words of the author, this book recounts how a biblical law, clear and direct, to protect the poor, a law that did not however take into account commercial loans, if followed exactly, could have brought commercial activities among Jews to a standstill. Through inventive interpretation, generations of rabbis essentially annulled the biblical ban and thus gave permission for business life to flourish.

While other studies or books have dealt with individual, specific parts of this development at various times or in various communities or in various particular circumstances or on the subject of particular means and instruments dealing with questions of interest, no other work prior to Gamoran's has followed this process in its manifold aspects from the biblical texts to our own time, in one study, under one cover. The bibliography of relevant primary and secondary sources on the subject of interest, *ribbit,* is exhaustive. The careful footnoting of the sources reveal Gamoran's mastery of a great variety of developments on the subject throughout the course of Jewish history.

The book is also a demonstration of the flexibility of Jewish religious law and its processes in confronting the overwhelming economic shift from biblical agrarian economies to the economies of complex commercial business enterprise; from the time when the lending of funds or commodities was for the purpose of sustaining the suffering poor to a time when the borrowing and lending on interest was an economic necessity.

Gamoran begins with a thorough explanation, in historic context, of each of the biblical versions of the law forbidding interest (Exod. 22:24; Lev. 25:35–37; Deut. 23:20–21) considering the items to be borrowed, the status of the borrower, and the terms for "interest" referred to in each of the different biblical texts. He then turns to the instruments of the more economically complex period of the Tannaim; the rabbis plugging one hole after another with restrictive legislation that prohibited usury in many new forms; then, facing market conditions unknown in biblical times, nullifying the very prohibitions that they themselves had instituted in order to enable Jews simply to make a living. He demonstrates how this process continued throughout our history. From this we gain a very practical insight into the concerns, issues, realities, and status of Jewish life in the various circumstances in which Jews lived.

Without a trace of the simplistic or the superficial, Gamoran is able lucidly to render the technical complexities of the "dismal science" of economics, at times making its mechanisms as interesting as the resolution of a fascinating puzzle. This is accomplished through a careful organization of the book around five major areas already foundational in early Rabbinic times such as: (1) loans of produce; (2) advance payment for the purchase of goods, which indeed amounted to lending money to a vendor; (3) buying on credit where the seller lends his goods to a buyer who delays payment; (4) mortgages where the lender receives the property of the borrower as security for his loan; and (5) investments where money given to the recipient is used to engage in business enterprise.

Further development of each of these types of transactions and others are shown in each historic period, from the Tannaim (ca. 70–200 C.E.), the Amoraim (ca. 200–500 C.E.), the period of the Geonim (ca. 650–1050), the Rishonim (ca. 1000–1500), and the Aharonim (ca. 1500–2000). Through the author's explanations and with the help of a clearly stated glossary of technical terms, we follow the process from beginning to end.

In this respect the book is far more than a discussion of one particular topic in the field of economics. It encapsulates a very important component in the entire economic history of the Jews. Focusing on this component also makes of the book an eye-opening treatise on the actual workings of Jewish law over many centuries, including glimpses into the sensibilities of particular rabbinic authorities.

But grounding it all, the springboard of the book is Rabbi Gamoran's moral consciousness:

> When I first began to study the subject, I was intrigued by the biblical injunction [prohibiting interest] because of its ethical mandate; it represented the highest form of morality, the rich caring for the poor, forbidding the exploitation of the unfortunate. But I soon became aware that the Halakhah has changed drastically since biblical days. Interest charges, completely forbidden in Scripture, are now openly allowed by the rabbinic authorities. How did a law of such high moral standing collapse and fall over the course of the centuries? This was my question and this is what I have set out to answer in the book. (p. 1)

This book is indeed an answer to the question. It is at the same time a document of appreciation of the capaciousness, the inherent flexibility, of the Jewish legal process that enabled devout Jewish communities to survive economically while remaining true to their faith. As Gamoran puts it, "the rabbis showed their initiative and inventiveness. On the one hand they were bound by their faith and training to uphold the laws of the Torah. The people lived in a credit society. To abandon interest would imperil their livelihoods. The rabbis...followed the path laid out by their predecessors... through bold interpretation of the Law...." It is a story, then, of how not only the livelihood of a people and thus their life itself endured, but also how a faith endured. Fitting the capaciousness of the Jewish tradition itself, Rabbi

Gamoran has brought a special capacity to tell this economic story, which is at the same time a story of Jewish history and of the Jewish spirit.

HERBERT BRONSTEIN (C57) is rabbi emeritus/senior scholar of North Shore Congregation Israel, Glencoe, Illinois, and a lecturer in History of Religions at Lake Forest College.

An Unsettling God: The Heart of the Hebrew Bible
by Walter Brueggemann
(Minneapolis: Fortress Press, 2009), 212 pp.

I first "discovered" Walter Brueggemann three years ago as I was doing research for my new book on Jeremiah. This distinguished biblical scholar and Christian theologian who is a prodigious writer (and is not slowing down now that he is retired) has written several fascinating books on the subject. We have since struck up an online friendship and I have been duly humbled by this man's charm and erudition.

In his new book, *An Unsettling God: The Heart of the Hebrew Bible*, the author distills his lifelong encounter with the Hebrew Bible and with contemporary theology, both Jewish and Christian, and tackles what is perhaps theology's most difficult question, namely, the nature of God. Having just spent three years studying Jeremiah's understanding of the nature of God, I have found this new book both enlightening and inspirational. As a Jew, I am awed by this prominent Christian theologian's deep respect for my biblical and contemporary heritage, giving credit where credit is due, and his admirable tact in not imposing his own belief system and heritage upon it. I see here a solid basis for understanding and rapprochement between our two faiths.

Brueggemann finds God, to whom he refers as YHWH, in a relationship born of an encounter between the human and the Divine. In this he is invoking Martin Buber, to whom he gives full credit. This in itself is not new, but what is new is the way he presents the four categories that sum up the nature of God. Those are: Israel, the nations, creation, and the individual human being. The author sees these four as "partners" with the Divine. Let us examine how the author tackles each category.

Israel

The author sees YHWH as first entering into a relationship with Israel:

> ...the distinctiveness of "God" in Old Testament tradition concerns YHWH's deep resolve to be a God *in relation*—in relation to Israel, in relation to creation, in relation to members of the Israelite society and of the human community more generally. The power and sovereignty of YHWH is a given in the Old Testament that is rarely called into question. What is readily and often called into question in the text is the character of this God *in relation*, a defining mark of YHWH that requires a radical revision of our notion of God. (p. 4)

The Nations

The relation between God and Israel results in the covenant between the two. Brueggemann sees this covenant as extended later on to the rest of humankind, but he rejects Paul's idea of the gospel of Jesus Christ replacing the law of Moses. He writes:

> I suggest that grace must also be subsumed under covenant. Covenant is the larger, working category through which this witness understands its life with YHWH, which entails a full relationship of self-giving and self-regarding in which embrace of commandments (in obedience) and embrace of love (in trust) are of a piece. (p.25)

Creation

Israel and, by extension, the human race, can find the generosity and the abundance of the Divine in creation, which is seen by Brueggemann as both physical and spiritual. In the Priestly construct of the tabernacle in Exodus 25–31 the author sees a parallel to the six days of creation, representing the physical universe, and the seventh day of rest, representing the spiritual dimension, as evidenced by the instructions given by YHWH to Moses in seven speeches (p. 142). Brueggemann appears to accept the widely held view that creation became a crucial claim of Israel's faith in exile, when Genesis 1:1–2:4a is commonly dated. He goes on to explain that in the chaotic and dangerous world of the exile, Israel found order and stability in its belief in a creation governed by a just and caring God, with whom Israel saw itself as a partner in perfecting the world (*tikkun olam*).

The Individual Person

The author provides a fourth partner with YHWH apart from the people Israel and the nations as collectives of people, namely, the individual person. Here we are told that the Hebrew Bible sees the humanness of the individual person as flowing from the humanness of the covenanted Israelite, not because the latter is superior to the former, but because the biblical author operates within the framework of the covenant between God and Israel (p. 58). Great emphasis is placed on the concept of human beings created "in the image of God":

> Reference to the image of God in Gen 5:1 and 9:6 affirms that the "primal sin" of the first couple ("the fall") does not deny to all subsequent humanity the character of the image of God. (p. 59)

Since both Brueggemann and I have devoted a great deal of time and effort to studying the teachings of Jeremiah and writing about them, I would like to give the foregoing the so-called "Jeremiah test." I would dare say that Jeremiah would agree with Brueggemann's fourfold presentation. The prophet's starting point in his prophetic career is the idea of the covenant between God and Israel: "I remember the kindness of your youth...your going after me in a land not sown" (2:2). From here all else flows. At the same time, when God is first revealed to the boy Jeremiah, the youngster is told: "I put you in charge of nations and kingdoms" (1:10). Throughout his career, Jeremiah concerns himself not only with his own people but with all the nations of his time and their relationship to the one God of the universe (especially as seen in his later prophecies to the nations). As for creation, from the first moment God reveals himself to the prophet and shows him the blossoming almond tree, Jeremiah will continue to commune with the Divine through nature, where he will repeatedly hear the voice of God. Finally, Jeremiah is the first prophet in the Bible who establishes the concept of the personal relationship between God and the individual person, when he challenges the traditional belief of children paying for the sins of their parents (31:29). In my book on Jeremiah I argue that here we have the turning point in biblical history, when the Judeans, about to go into Babylonian exile, begin to realize that God is not tribal or territorial, but rather universal and directly connected to each individual human being.

Another important point that indeed passes this test is Brueggemann's rejection of the traditional Christian belief that while Judaism is the religion of law, Christianity is the religion of love. Jeremiah teaches us of a God who is passionately in love with his people who break his covenant and hence face severe punishment. The underlying message of the book of Jeremiah is that both love and law are indeed part and parcel of the covenant.

I am grateful to Brueggemann for writing this book. This important work can go a long way in helping both Jews and others better understand the relation between the human and the Divine.

RABBI MORDECAI SCHREIBER (NY65) is the author of the new book *The Man Who Knew God: Decoding Jeremiah.*

The Sights Along the Harbor
by Harvey Shapiro
(Middletown, CT: Wesleyan University Press, 2006), 253 pp.

The high quality of Harvey Shapiro's poems in his many books has been well established. His credentials are many and include being on the staffs of both *Commentary* and *The New Yorker*. He was an editor of the *New York Times Magazine* and the editor of the *New York Times Book Review*. (By the way, he is not to be confused with Karl Shapiro, who also served in World War II and wrote many poems of Jewish interest.) Others have reviewed the quality of this book. (For example, see www.nytimes.com/2006/03/12/books/review/12barber.html.) So, instead of reviewing the poems as poems, I will turn to the question of what in his work would be of interest to the Jewish experience.

In *The Sights Along the Harbor*, Shapiro, who was born in a Yiddish-speaking household in 1924, includes new poems along with selections from his ten books of poetry. Of those many poems, he touches on the Jewish experience in more than forty, which shows how acutely aware he is of his identity. Further, he does not hesitate to say so in print, which is notable since a number of these poems were published at a time when literary figures were not always vocal about their Jewish identity. He is clearly a man who wrestles with Jewish life.

Nevertheless, he is not uncritical. In "God Poem," he tells us that, "Nobody does silence as well as God." Or even more critical, in "In the Synagogue," he writes, "The new year. Five thousand what?/In his scrolls, with touches of/Megalomania and song." In "Loyalty," he speaks about his commitment to the Jewish people despite its history and despite God's silence. He writes, "They have been driven insane by history,/my tribe…God can forsake them, whenever./Hasn't He?/He has the option./I don't." Shapiro has a profound sense of the horror of the Shoah and God's silence. Listen to "Ditty:"

> Where did the Jewish god go?
> Up the chimney flues.
> Who saw him go?
> Six million souls.
> How did he go?
> All so still
> As dew from the grass.

Shapiro not only sees the Shoah as a failure of God but also the failure of Western culture. In "ABC of Culture," he says, "So the angel of death whistles Mozart/(As we knew he would)/Bicycling amid the smoke of Auschwitz,/The Jews of Auschwitz,/In the great museum of Western Art." And yet in "The Generations," he says that even though the father swaying while holding his baby may not go to shul as had his father, "the prayer that bound them all/was still being said."

Shapiro shows both his sense of humor and his ability to humanize biblical figures. In "Adam," he speculates,

> It is possible Adam
> was bored in paradise,
> the leafy green settling,
> in his mind like fog.
> I have a taste for something
> else, he thought, but what?

Shapiro is acutely conscious of living in two worlds. In "Brooklyn Heights," he notes, "In this corner of the world/live two traditions, four dead poets." Then he mentions both Whitman and Zukofsky, "All walking/where the ferryboats sparkle."

He clearly loves Israel. In "A Jerusalem Notebook," he says, "Give me this place for my own,/I cried, and I will live here forever./The prospect is as sweet/as a Sabbath morning." But he understands that it is a real place with real people. Later in the same poem he observes, "Blondes from Scandinavia,/silver-toed, tried on Arab dresses/while the man in the stall scratched his crotch."

He has a humorous view of an afterlife. In "Jerusalem," he concludes,

> At the end of time
> will I be with the other Jews
> crowding the narrow entrance
> of the El Al gate,
> cleared for takeoff
> from New York to Tel Aviv.

I could go on and on with his take on Jewish life and his place in it, but these few excerpts should be enough to show you a man with a sense of humor who wrestles with Jewish life. His book is well worth the time and, who knows, there may even be material here that can be used in sermons or teaching.

ADAM D. FISHER (NY67) is rabbi emeritus of Temple Isaiah, Stony Brook, New York, and poetry editor of the *CCAR Journal*.

The Modern Men's Torah Commentary: New Insights from Jewish Men on the 54 Weekly Torah Portions
Edited by Rabbi Jeffrey K. Salkin
(Woodstock, VT: Jewish Lights, 2009), 368 pp.

I was skeptical when I first heard that Jewish Lights was going to be releasing a Torah commentary from a man's point of view. Why do we need that? Don't we have plenty of that already? The proud feminist in me cried out: if we're going to invest in a Torah study project that approaches the text with an emphasis on gender, shouldn't we augment the growing (but still by comparison, miniscule)[1] *women's* Torah commentary corpus? The answer is a resounding yes. Five books do not a library make. Even if one were to account for the many other fine volumes in the field of Jewish feminism (thankfully too numerous for me to footnote!), it would still not be *dayeinu*. The voices of our mothers and daughters have been marginalized (or worse, silenced) since time immemorial. As we realize this, our generation has a responsibility to do all it can to begin making up for that dearth by raising up feminist-minded (female *and* male) students who will be able to fill the void by writing, teaching, and ultimately speaking out loud words that our tradition has quieted for far too long.

What I have come to appreciate, as I have spent time learning from and enjoying *The Modern Men's Torah Commentary* (edited by Jeffrey Salkin, to whom credit goes for assembling such a Jewishly diverse group of teachers), is that its title is both apt and misleading. Apt because, indeed, it does seek to be "a Torah commentary that would open men up to the life of Torah and teach them how the life of Torah intersects with their own lives" (p. xv). In this sense, *The Modern Men's Torah Commentary* is a handy reference for Jewish (and non-Jewish) men. There is ample discussion by its (male) contributors, who offer essays on the *parashiyot* about the challenges of being a father, a son, and a provider. (It goes without saying that the themes, messages, and texts are all *chomer lidrush* for us to use in any number of rabbinic settings.)

But the book's title is misleading, because I was struck by the fact that the book is so much more than *just* a meditation on issues facing Jewish men today. Although it is a *chiddush* that this volume ties those insights to the *parashah*, there are other volumes that one could turn to if one was interested in exploring Jewish men's issues today.[2] What is really unique about *The Modern Men's Torah Commentary* is that it uses men's issues as a lens to creatively examine a number of the challenges facing the entirety of the Jewish community today. Here are just a few highlights:

In empathizing with Jacob's "burden" of being chosen over Esau, Julius Lester (a welcome addition as one of the few lay contributors to the anthology) considers the dynamics of his own family-of-origin, all the while weaving together potent observations about race and class. He writes:

> I was born in 1939, at a time when racial segregation was the accepted norm. I grew up in the black community of Kansas City, Kansas, which was so separate from white communities that my

> only contact with whites came in stores. Up to the age of fourteen, I can recall having spoken with only one white person—my piano teacher—for a brief period.
>
> Segregation gave white people an almost absolute power over black lives. Though we lived in fear of that power, we also believed that one day things would be different, and when that day came, we had to be prepared.
>
> I do not know what it was my father and teachers saw in me, but they saw something and chose me as one of those they would arm to do battle with white society's oppressive power (p. 58).

Lester's story becomes bigger than his own unique (and important) family drama. Its inclusion invites us to honor Lester's own struggles, and it reminds us of the remarkable texture and diversity that populates our community today, at a time when more than 10 percent of all American Jews are non-white.[3] More importantly, Lester's contribution invites us to make his story our own. Haven't some of our parents and grandparents looked to us to get an education, in order to stand up and make a name for our (Jewish) selves in the world, to take advantage of opportunities that they never had? Indeed, that pressure to achieve a certain standing of social and economic success has come with its tradeoffs: namely that of assimilation, a result of the immigration process that we rabbis continue to wrestle with, nearly a century after the massive wave of Eastern European immigration to this country ended.

The Modern Men's Torah Commentary also stakes out new ground in offering us a franker discussion about sexuality. (Although Meszler and Salkin both explore sexuality in the volumes that they penned on Jewish men, one gets the distinct feeling that they were both aiming to appeal to a hetero audience.)

Joel Lurie Grishaver speculates on Joseph's sexuality and its connection to his masculinity. Citing Thomas Mann, Grishaver suggests that Joseph's coat of many colors is evidence that Joseph is "the first metrosexual" of the Bible (p. 63). Later, Grishaver describes Joseph just before the big "reveal" scene (Gen. 45) of being dressed in "Egyptian 'drag'" (p. 65). It's not much, but it's a step forward in our commentators' willingness to dip their toes into the waters of queer theory as we seek to interpret Torah anew.[4]

More interesting is Steven Greenberg's essay on *Acharei Mot*. (He humorously opens his piece by writing: "In gay Jewish terms, *Acharei Mot* is the 'scene of the crime'" (p. 170) because it includes two of the Torah's three prohibitions against gay male sex.) The essay is partially a rehash of the kind of material Greenberg presented in his important work *Wrestling with God and Men: Homosexuality in the Jewish Tradition*. He explores the Torah's silence on lesbianism, and then brings his own analysis to bear on the halachic question at hand. After discussing several texts, he concludes:

> Consequently, sexual relations that occur without violence or humiliation, that are not part of the dramaturgy of pagan rites but are marked by intimacy and love, care and commitment, ought to be permissible.

> While these two contexts may seem a bit extreme or historically distant at first blush, we should not be too quick to dismiss them. There are manifestations of public or group sex in certain gay circles that are not so far from the pagan dramaturgy described by Rabbi Ishmael. The link between sex and power is even more common. Is there not an anarchic lure for men toward sexuality as an expression of power? (p. 174)

Greenberg skillfully uses his discussion about power to steer the conversation out of a strictly gay context and into the world of relationships in general, where every reader, regardless of sexual orientation, will surely be able to identify with him. Thus he concludes:

> In the medieval sex guide *The Letter of Holiness*, Rabbi Moses ben Nachman (Ramban or Nachmanides) instructs that a husband ought to seduce his wife but never force her. How should a man navigate the line between seduction and force? Must "no" always mean "no" between married partners? According to the *halachah* (Jewish law), finding the line between playful and intrusive aggression is best determined by the receiver. If sex can easily slip into abuse or (more commonly) boredom, then the only way to navigate the dangerous and fickle waters is to achieve a high degree of awareness and communication between partners. The challenge is to find a way to keep sex intimate and relational while leaving room for mystery, risk, and play so that we create a reliably renewable excitement that fulfills the common human desire to be repeatedly overwhelmed—by love. (p. 175)

BOOK REVIEWS

Power, and the question of the Jewishly responsible exercising of it, is also at the heart of the essay that moved me the most, written by Danny Landes (who lives in Jerusalem) on *Ki Teitzei*. Responding to *v'shavita shivyo* (Deut. 21:10), Landes translates and then explains:

> "And you shall take some of them captive"; literally, "and you shall capture him as a captive." This double use of "capture/captive" (*shavita/shivyo*) refers reflexively to the double capture that our sons endure. By holding the other in captivity, they are also captured. They are in the dual captivity of their own "attack mentality" and their own *menschlichkeit*—both of which we, parents and teachers, have evoked and demanded. The loss of either one of these qualities would spell disaster—physical and moral—for both them and for the nation [the State of Israel]. Can they be kept in balance? Yes, there is a tension. But the nature of people, situations, and struggle, renders all of this to be a dynamic tension. (p. 286)

Landes goes on to relay two stories of moral crisis relating to IDF service: one, told to him by a devoted former student, about the daily humiliation (for both soldier and Palestinian) of forcing Palestinians to strip (to insure that there are no explosives strapped to their body) before allowing them to cross into Israel. The other story, told by Landes's son, is about the choice of ignoring curfew rules to allow a seemingly innocent Palestinian doctor be with his family. Fascinatingly, Landes seeks to resolve these questions by employing the Jewish semantics of gender. Thus he concludes:

> What would you or I have decided, in these rather simple occurrences, which contain so much moral weight and ambivalence? Making those decisions in real split-second time creates an instant pull between the dual "attack" and *menschlichkeit* mentalities. In the end, it's a man's job, and I honor those who have to make those decisions.
>
> *Ki tetzei*—"when you go out": they deserve that we empathetically go out with them to the danger—existential and moral. (p. 287)

When Landes writes that "it's a man's job," I would like to think that he wasn't referring to male IDF soldiers per se (after all, so many Israeli women proudly serve in the IDF as well). What I think he meant is that we (Jewish men and women) aspire to a kind of ideal Jewishness—a Jewishness that is equally transgressive of the gender roles that both men and women are so often forced to embrace.

For men, *menschlichkeit* is one way out of that. Jewish values provide us with an opportunity to evolve beyond the Spike TV stereotypical presentation of our gender. We are more than cigar-smoking poker players. And we are more than overgrown, womanizing frat boys.

For women, feminism is one way out from the inherited gender roles that you have inherited. Jewish feminism provides you with a context to evolve beyond the Lifetime: Television for Women stereotypical presentation of your gender. You are more than the objects of a deranged lover's affections. And you are more than a character in a ridiculously unrealistic makeover fantasy.

In realizing this, we might appreciate how successful Salkin was in situating his project—a *men's* Torah commentary—not outside of the bounds of feminism, but directly within it.[5]

Notes

1. Sadly, miniscule is an understatement. In terms of commentaries that seek to be comprehensive, by addressing the themes of every Torah portion, we have: Ellen Frankel's playful and creative *Five Books of Miriam* (Grosset/Putnam); Judith Antonelli's less well-known *In the Image of God: A Feminist Commentary on the Torah* (Jason Aronson); *The Women's Torah Commentary* (Jewish Lights) (and its companion Haftarah/Five Megillot volume) by Elyse Goldstein; and, of course, the groundbreaking *The Torah: A Women's Commentary* (URJ Press) by Tamara Cohn Eskenazi and Andrea Weiss.

2. Our colleague Joseph Meszler has written *A Man's Responsibility: A Jewish Guide to Being a Son, a Partner in Marriage, a Father, and a Community Leader* (Jewish Lights). And Salkin himself wrote *Searching for My Brothers: Jewish Men in a Gentile World* (Putnam). I enjoyed spending time with both of these volumes, and I consider them useful companion volumes to *The Modern Men's Torah Commentary*.

3. See, for example, http://bechollashon.org/.

4. For more, see Robert Goss and Mona West, eds., *Take Back the Word: A Queer Reading of the Bible* (Cleveland: Pilgrim Press, 2000).

5. See p. xvi.

JEFFREY BROWN (C05) is associate rabbi at Temple Solel, Cardiff, California.

BOOK REVIEWS

The Passionate Torah: Sex and Judaism
Edited by Danya Ruttenberg
(New York and London: New York University Press, 2009), 320 pp.

Well, they tell ya, "Don't judge a book by its cover," and that is certainly the case with *The Passionate Torah: Sex and Judaism*, edited by Rabbi Danya Ruttenberg. An unmade bed with ruffled sheets dons the cover. It grabs your attention. But make no mistake, this book is not easy.

The Passionate Torah is comprised of eighteen essays written by serious scholars, rabbis, and activists including Aryeh Cohen, Elliot Dorff, Melanie Malka Landau, Laura Levitt, Naomi Seidman, Sarra Lev, Rabbi Dr. Haviva Ner-David, and Elliot Kukla. Each of the authors uses the tools and lenses of contemporary academic discourse—postmodernism, queer theory, feminism, political theory, and gay spirituality—to critique and challenge Jewish tradition and Rabbinic texts as they pertain to sexuality and sexual relationships of all kinds. The authors discuss and challenge biblical and Rabbinic concepts such as the sotah, nidah, prostitution, non-marital sexual relations, b'tulah/zonah, and even masturbation.

In the essay "Love the One You're With," Laura Levitt strives to understand what a radical vision of the erotic might mean to feminists today. She builds a bridge from the feminist poet Audrey Lorde through the Jewish feminist theologian Judith Plaskow to political theorist Marla Brettschneider (influenced by Martin Buber). Levitt compellingly challenges the institutions of marriage and monogamy and suggests alternative significant relationships.

In Jay Michaelson's essay, "On the Religious Significance of Homosexuality; or, Queering God, Torah, and Israel," he asks, "Is being gay like having brown eyes—a biological quirk of no religious significance? Or, given the central status in Judaism of procreation, patrimony, and gender binarism, is there something more theologically significant about people who, because of their souls' anatomies, defy the traditional constructions of each? And if there is something significant about GLBT people, what is it?" In answering these questions, Michaelson refers to contemporary queer theory and contemporary gay spirituality—two discourses that typically do not interact with each other or our rabbinical school curriculum.

In Haviva Ner-David's essay, "Reclaiming Nidah and Mikveh through Ideological and Practical Reinterpretation," the author supports couples' practicing the sexual regimen of nidah (periodic sexual separation within marriage) and mikveh. She contends that it can bring a couple closer together. At the same time, she notes it would be irresponsible to do so without making changes to one's actual praxis so that it reflects and is consistent with one's ideolgical viewpoint. Ner-David, a self-identified Orthodox Jew, encourages couples to stress the ritual's potential to strengthen the marital bond and not to focus on the idea of women's impure bodies. Ner-David references many Talmudic texts and quotes Rabbi Meir (BT Nidah 31b) in support of her position.

Danya Ruttenberg's essay asks, "How can we begin to talk about women's bodies and clothing, as well as the notion of tzniut in a broader sense, in a way that emphasizes the importance of our erotic, integrated, Divinely connected selves rather than focusing on compartmentalized individual body parts. What would it mean to get dressed as a subject?"

This is a question that occupied our Sages and can and should occupy our communities today as girls and boys are continually confronted with provocatively dressed individuals at schools, in music videos, and even at temple.

As my experience working with university students at the University of Chicago, Columbia University, and the American Jewish World Service suggests, the questions that these distinguished authors raise are important for rabbis to ponder as they are precisely the questions and the discourse that many of our youth confront each day in academia.

RABBI RUTH GELFARB (NY07) most recently worked as the senior Jewish educator at the University of Chicago's Newberger Hillel Center.

The CCAR Journal: The Reform Jewish Quarterly
Published quarterly by the Central Conference of American Rabbis.

Volume LVII, No. 1. Issue Number: Two hundred twenty-three.
Winter 2010.

STATEMENT OF PURPOSE

The CCAR Journal: The Reform Jewish Quarterly seeks to explore ideas and issues of Judaism and Jewish life, primarily—but not exclusively—from a Reform Jewish perspective. To fulfill this objective, the Journal is designed to:

1. provide a forum to reflect the thinking of informed and concerned individuals—especially Reform rabbis—on issues of consequence to the Jewish people and the Reform Movement;

2. increase awareness of developments taking place in fields of Jewish scholarship and the practical rabbinate, and to make additional contributions to these areas of study;

3. encourage creative and innovative approaches to Jewish thought and practice, based upon a thorough understanding of the traditional sources.

The views expressed in the Journal do not necessarily reflect the position of the Editorial Board or the Central Conference of American Rabbis.

The CCAR Journal: The Reform Jewish Quarterly (ISSN 1058-8760) is published quarterly by the Central Conference of American Rabbis, 355 Lexington Avenue, 18th Floor, New York, NY, 10017. Application to mail at periodical postage rates is pending at New York, NY and at additional mailing offices.

Subscriptions should be sent to CCAR Executive Offices, 355 Lexington Avenue, 18th Floor, New York, NY, 10017. Subscription rate as set by the Conference is $75 for a one-year subscription, $125 for a two-year subscription. Overseas subscribers should add $36 per year for postage. POSTMASTER: Please send address changes to The CCAR Journal: The Reform Jewish Quarterly, c/o Central Conference of American Rabbis, 355 Lexington Avenue, 18th Floor, New York, NY, 10017.

Typesetting and publishing services provided by Publishing Synthesis, Ltd., 39 Crosby Street, New York, NY, 10013.

The CCAR Journal: The Reform Jewish Quarterly is indexed in the *Index to Jewish Periodicals*. Articles appearing in it are listed in the *Index of Articles on Jewish Studies* (of *Kirjath Sepher*).

© Copyright 2010 by the Central Conference of American Rabbis.
All rights reserved.
ISSN 1058-8760

ISBN: 978-0-88123-156-4

GUIDELINES FOR SUBMITTING MATERIAL

1. The *CCAR Journal* welcomes submissions that fulfill its Statement of Purpose whatever the author's background or identification. Inquiries regarding publishing in the CCAR Journal and submissions for possible publication (including poetry) should be sent to the editor, Rabbi Susan Laemmle, in electronic form via <u>Laemmle@usc.edu</u>. Should problems arise, call 323-939-4084.

2. Other than commissioned articles, submissions to the *CCAR Journal* are sent out to a member of the editorial board for anonymous peer review. Thus submitted articles and poems should be sent to the editor with the author's name omitted. Please use MS Word format for the attachment. The message itself should contain the author's name, phone number, and e-mail address, as well as the submission's title and a 1–2 sentence bio.

3. Based on Reform Judaism's commitment to egalitarianism, we request that articles be written in gender-inclusive language.

4. Books for review and inquiries regarding submitting a review should be sent directly to the book review editor, Rabbi Laurence Edwards, at <u>Laurenceedwards@sbcglobal.net</u>.

5. The *Journal* publishes reference notes at the end of articles, but submissions are easier to review when notes come at the bottom of each page. If possible, keep this in mind when submitting an article. Notes should conform to the following style:

   a. Norman Lamm, *The Shema: Spirituality and Law in Judaism* (Philadelphia: Jewish Publication Society, 1998), 101–6. **[book]**

   b. Lawrence A. Hoffman, "The Liturgical Message," in *Gates of Understanding*, ed. Lawrence A.Hoffman (New York: CCAR Press, 1977), 147–48, 162–63. **[chapter in a book]**

   c. Richard Levy, "The God Puzzle," *Reform Judaism* 28 (Spring 2000): 18–22. **[article in a periodical]**

   d. Lamm, *Shema*, 102. **[short form for subsequent reference]**

   e. Levy, "God Puzzle," 20. **[short form for subsequent reference]**

   f. Ibid., 21. **[short form for subsequent reference]**

6. If Hebrew script is used, please include an English translation. If transliteration is used, follow the guidelines abbreviated below and included more fully in the **Master Style Sheet**, available on the CCAR website at <u>www.ccarnet.org</u>:

   "ch" for *chet* and *chaf*   "ei" for *tzeirei*
   "f" for *fei*   "a" for *patach* and *kamatz*
   "k" for *kaf* and *kuf*   "o" for *cholam* and *kamatz katan*
   "tz" for *tzadi*   "u" for *shuruk* and *kibbutz*
   "i" for *chirik*   "ai" for *patach* with *yod*
   "e" for *segol*

   Final "h" for final *hei*; none for final *ayin* (with exceptions based on common usage): *atah*, *Sh'ma*, <u>but</u> *Moshe*.

   Apostrophe for *sh'va nah*: *b'nei*, *b'rit*, *Sh'ma*; no apostrophe for *sh'va nach*.

   Hyphen for two vowels together where necessary for correct pronunciation: *ne-eman*, *samei-ach*, <u>but</u> *maariv*, Shavuot.

   No hyphen for prefixes unless necessary for correct pronunciation: *babayit*, HaShem, Yom HaAtzma-ut.

   Do not double consonants (with exceptions based on dictionary spelling or common usage): *t'filah*, *chayim*, <u>but</u> *tikkun*, Sukkot.

www.ingramcontent.com/pod-product-compliance
Lightning Source LLC
Chambersburg PA
CBHW050643160426
43194CB00010B/1792